The Friendly City—
TOXIC TERRAIN

By Antonio Richardson

Editing and Design by Susana M. Choy

CONTENTS

Acknowledgments

I would like to give special thanks to Anna H. Oshiro JD.
Additionally, I would like to thank my editor Susana Choy
for her hard work and diligence. My mother, Sarah E. Richardson,
provided me with support throughout the writing of this book
by visiting the Columbus-Lowndes Public library in search of
material about Morningside Apartments.
Bettye Browne's services at the library were indispensable.
I also want to express gratitude to my dear sisters
Sereta Richardson and Lori Wilson. Thank you to my
longtime friend Jerry "Terrell" Petty for his ongoing support
and agreeing to being interviewed. As well I want to thank
Eric Collins and Sherita Deloach for agreeing to be interviewed
long distance. Their cooperation is greatly appreciated.

Housing and Urban Act of 1965

The Housing and Urban Development Act of 1965 was the most ambitious federal housing effort undertaken since the Housing Act of 1949. The 1965 act extended the urban renewal programs set in motion by the 1949 act, which provided various forms of federal assistance to cities for removing dilapidated housing and redeveloping parts of downtowns around the country.

The act also extended the code enforcement program, which required that cities enact a code specifying minimum standards for housing before they could participate in the urban renewal program. In addition, the act, which initiated or extended the Federal Housing Administration's mortgage-insurance programs, enabled more American families to purchase a home.

The basis for the act is Congress's taxing and spending power as stated in the U.S. Constitution, Article I, Section 8, which authorizes the legislature to provide for the general welfare.

The most controversial and innovative part of the act, however, created a rent-supplement program whereby qualified tenants paid 25 percent of their income in rent and the program paid the balance directly to the housing provider. The supplement ceased when the occupant was able to pay their rent in full. To qualify, an individual's income had to be within the set limits for public housing eligibility and they had to be either elderly, physically handicapped, displaced by a public-improvement program, living in substandard housing or occupying housing damaged by a natural disaster. Only private, nonprofit or, in some cases, limited-profit corporations were eligible housing sponsors.

It is important to note that in 1973 President Nixon halted funding for the rent-supplement program. Ultimately, it was replaced by what is now commonly known as the Section 8 program. This often-amended rent-supplement program is an essential component of the Housing and Community Development Act of 1974 that authorizes subsidies of a tenant's rent in privately-owned housing.

History of Fair Housing

On April 11, 1968 President Lyndon Johnson signed the Civil Rights Act
of 1968, a follow up to the Civil Rights Act of 1964. This piece of legislation expanded on previous acts and prohibited discrimination regarding
the rentals and financing of residential housing property based on race,
religion, national origin, sex, handicap and family status. It was also
known as Title VIII or the Fair Housing Act of 1968. A significant bill, it
mandated more homes for black Americans. Until the passage of the Fair
Housing Act, the vast majority of new housing was being built for white
people while black people often lived in tin shacks with no electricity,
running toilets or running water.

The enactment of the bill came only after a long and difficult journey.
From 1966 to 1967, Congress regularly considered the passage of the
Fair Housing Bill, but every vote failed to get close to a majority for it to
become law. A racist Congress did not want the bill approved.

Vietnam War veterans felt the lack of decent housing most acutely. Poor
black American infantrymen returned home from the war and could
not purchase or rent homes for their families in many neighborhoods.
Senator Edward Brooke III, the first black American ever to be elected to
the U.S. Senate spoke of his return from World War II and his inability to
provide a home of his choice for his young family because of his race.

Senator Brooke III pushed for the passage of the Fair Housing Bill, but
it took the assassination of Dr. Martin Luther King, Jr. and the resulting
black riots across the country to move Congress to act. Without debate,
Congress unanimously passed the Fair Housing Act overnight. President
Johnson promptly signed the bill and it became law.

PART I

Morningside Apartments

CHAPTER ONE

Morningside Apartments

I was seven years old when my family moved from the south side to the north side of Columbus, Mississippi. It was the summer of 1970 and Morningside Apartments[1] was a brand new $1.5 million rent supplemented complex. The Fair Housing Act had created the opportunity for the complex to be built. It was the second of its type in the state of Mississippi and it was privately owned. The first Morningside Apartment complex was corporate-owned and located in Greenville, Mississippi.

Our Morningside complex was a 10-acre site at 1802 25th Street North (later renamed Martin Luther King Jr. Drive). It was a 12-building complex, three of which were small single-story buildings with office space. The 120 apartment units that made up the remainder of the complex were comprised of eight one-bedroom, 60 two-bedroom, 48 three-bedroom, and four four-bedroom apartments. Each unit boasted an electric range, a refrigerator, vinyl asbestos floors and ceramic tile bathrooms. In one corner of the landscaped grounds was a children's playground.

My parents had waited until the summer months before moving to Morningside Apartments to avoid disrupting our school year. Still, we made many changes and adjustments.

One morning my friend Terrell's mother visited. She was in my mother's room for a while and as she left she stopped to inform me that I had a new baby sister. I was very surprised and happy. At the time I was too young to realize that my mother was pregnant with our second sister. With her arrival we became a family of three boys and two girls.

I didn't know it then but the city hospital was not a place where Mississippi's black population wanted their children cared for — especially overnight — during the 1960s and early 1970s. Many blacks could not afford to have a hospital birth; furthermore throughout the black community, there were many stories of abuse and neglect of black infants by the City Hospital staff. Therefore, many older black women became midwives who delivered black infants safely and successfully.

---

1   Morningside Apartments was only one of several residential developments to be built on landfilled creosote. The EPA spent hundreds of millions of dollars to clean up a housing development at various housing complexes across the nation.

That fall, I attended Hughes Elementary School where I completed the second, third and fourth grades. It was within walking distance from the apartments — about three blocks. The elementary school had an unusually large playground with a long fence that separated the school grounds from a small lake.

My mother recently told me that Morningside Apartments was "the best we'd ever done" for ourselves during that era.

Even as a small child in the second grade I noticed some unusual activities with the daily goings-on within the new apartment complex. A noticeable problem was that all the water coming from any faucet on the premises, indoors or out, had a light brownish tinge. It was similar to the color of the water in Flint, Michigan during their water contamination crisis in 2016. You would have to let the hot or cold run for 10 to 20 seconds before it would run clear. Being a child I thought that the pipes were rusty even though the building complex was brand new.

Then, there were many "Keep off the Grass" signs on the premises. We wondered why anyone would place so many families with children in a large complex with nowhere for kids to play near their homes. The resident manager charged a hefty $20 fine if any child or adult walked on the grass for any reason.

We were all small kids and our parents did not allow us to go outside to play unless one of them was at home. I can remember being spanked numerous times for breaking this rule. Terrell and many of the other kids had no restrictions, so I made my parents aware that my older sister and I felt the rule was unfair. What was their answer to this? "We don't care how anyone else raises their kids." With restricted play times, I made sure I made the most of my time outside.

Terrell and I would often play at the Morningside playground that was located just one building away from ours. One of the regular features just beyond the playground was the creosote-covered telephone poles that were stacked on long, unhitched trailers. Terrell and I would often play on them, getting creosote all over our hands and clothes. We had no idea the poles were from the Kerr-McGee creosote plant. The plant stored these contaminated poles just beyond the playground after the poles were removed from their kiln. As a result, many of the children who

Playing next door on the Kerr-McGee property

lived in Morningside Apartments ended up playing on the creosote-covered wood.

Living in Morningside wasn't idyllic. Once or sometimes twice a week, we would be the recipients of a noxious odor that seemed to come from the Kerr-McGee kiln that cooked creosote into the telephone poles and rail road ties. This awful tar-like stench lingered in the air for most of any given day.

We moved out of Morningside Apartments in 1973 — sooner than my parents would have liked. This was primarily because the resident manager started charging for and enforcing an illegal $200 fine on my mother, and other specific residents, whenever he caught them walking on the grass. We got word that this was illegal and found out later that he was arrested for doing so.

From Morningside we moved back to the south side of Columbus. We stayed at my great aunt's house for a couple of weeks while we waited for our new rental to be vacated. I finished my elementary school years at Mitchell Memorial Elementary School where I averaged one fight a week. It wasn't due to anything I did. We were new and it seemed that that was just the way new kids were treated. We lived just a block away from the school and kids would follow me home just to pick a fight. The fights were almost a daily ritual during fifth grade at Mitchell Memorial. However, I hardly got into any fights in sixth grade. By that time everybody knew that I knew how to fight and that I wasn't going to run. If anyone wanted to fight me they were in for it.

My education continued at Hunt Jr. High School where I started the seventh grade. The school was located on the north side of Columbus, just behind the creosote plant; it has since closed due to contaminated grounds. Eighth grade found me at Joe Cook Jr. High School, situated about a half mile away from the same creosote plant also on the north side of Columbus. It too was closed due to contaminated grounds. My stepfather told me on several occasions that as a boy in the 1950s, he and his brothers would visit the north side of Columbus where much of the land had yet to be developed. At that time, the land where Morningside Apartments and the junior high schools now stand was covered with trees and what they called a "black lake." By the time the 1950s rolled around the creosote plant had already been operating for decades, having been opened in 1928 by the T. J. Moss Tie Company. It was a wood treatment plant that Kerr-McGee Chemical Corporation purchased in 1964. It produced treated railroad ties, switch ties, crossings and pilings using pentachlorophenol solution first and in 1976 switching to creosote as a preservative. The Kerr-McGee creosote plant occupied 90 acres in the middle of Columbus, Mississippi.

Though my stepfather was the only dad I ever knew, he never treated me like I was his son. He was often physically and verbally abusive with me and my older sister. I figured it was because we weren't "his" kids as were my three younger siblings. He also whipped us well into our teen-age years and I witnessed him taking a hand to my mom a couple times. He could be a mean son-of-a-gun. However, he did have his good points. He was a good provider, so we always had a roof over our heads, food in the fridge and we all attended church together. At the age of 15, tired of being beaten regularly, I told my mother that I no longer wanted to live with them. I wanted to move up north to the Chicago area to live with my mom's older sister, Emma. By this time my older sister had already moved out about three years prior to live with my grandmother who was also in Chicago. When my mom spoke with Emma about the situation, Emma — knowing what my stepdad was like — happily agreed to have me.

A couple of months later I left Columbus, Mississippi and moved to Harvey, Illinois to live with Emma and her husband, James. They were known to have fostered children, although there were none during my one-year stay. James was a church pastor and a high school teacher. He and I often commuted together to and from school unless I stayed at my aunt Kate's house in Chicago, where several of my first cousins lived.

Things were really good for a while, but once the luster of living in a new city settled, I realized my life there was very similar to my life back home. Life consisted of church and school and church hours were even longer than in Mississippi.

A year later, in 1979, my cousin, his girlfriend and I went to visit my mom in Columbus, Mississippi and I ended up staying for good. My stepfather was no longer physically abusive though he continued to be verbally abusive by berating me and trying to kill my spirit by telling me I wasn't going to amount to much. In Columbus, I went to high school for one semester before deciding to drop out. School no longer interested me and I cut classes a lot. When my mom found out she told me, "If you're going to go to school then go. If you're not going to go then don't go. But going sometimes and cutting classes is not the way to do it." At that point, I decided to take her words to heart and drop out of high school. I had found an after-school job at a Mexican restaurant during my first semester and having my own money and the ability to buy what I wanted felt good. So I started working full time at the restaurant, happy to have money and not concerning myself about the future.

At the restaurant, a fellow co-worker and classmate of mine, Michael, and I got into mischief. We often stole beer and Michael, having worked there a long time, had figured out how to do so without getting caught. The restaurant had a second floor where it was only used on weekends. When it wasn't used, it was closed off and the lights were turned off. When the restaurant was slow, I would crawl through the serving window into the closed off section and Michael would pass two empty beer pitchers to me on a bus pan. I would fill the pitchers from the tap, set them back on the bus pan and he would slide them back out of the serving window.

This all stopped after an incident at home. One night I had a little too much to drink at work and got drunk. The restaurant owner drove me home; she didn't realize I had stolen the alcohol from the restaurant. I walked in and realized I was hungry and needed the toilet. I started to head to the toilet but decided to stop at the refrigerator first to look for something to eat. I vaguely remember my mother walking past me and at some point I became confused and started to piss into the refrigerator. That's when I felt my mother knock me on the side of my head with something that shook me out of my confusion. I quickly stopped pissing and stumbled into my room, where I landed face down on my bed.

When I awoke I apologized to my mother and gave her money for new groceries. I realized that my drinking was eventually going to get me fired, so I stopped.

After spending four years with my parents in that house, my parents decided to buy a brand new home just two blocks away (where they reside to this day). One year later I moved in with my sister, Lori, to help her with her toddler and to enjoy more freedom. Her husband, Fred, had gone to basic training to join the Army Reserve. When he returned, my curiosity about his experience ate at me. I asked him about everything he'd experienced at the army's basic training. I wanted to know what it felt like, what he did, what he learned. He made it all sound so easy. I joined.

CHAPTER TWO

The U.S. Army

I signed up for the U.S. Army in 1981. I did my basic training at Fort Benning, Georgia from September through November with a one-week break for Thanksgiving. This was my introduction to real discipline. This would also be the first time that the anger that raged silently inside me would manifest itself outwardly.

One day, the drill sergeant yelled for a formation. On this day I was among the last to fall in and I broke ranks positioning myself between two other soldiers. We had our M16-A1 rifles stacked prior to falling into formation. I squeezed in between two of my fellow soldiers and managed not to get yelled at or dropped for push-ups. Once the formation was dismissed, one of the two soldiers I squeezed in between came up to me and gave me a hard push and said, "Richardson, if you ever break ranks with me again, I'll kick your butt." I had my weapon in my hands and without thinking I knocked him in the mouth with the butt of it. I also knocked a tooth out.

A small crowd had gathered and it caught the drill sergeant's attention. When he asked what happened I told him the truth. I said I reacted to what I viewed as an assault to my person. Consequently, I was denied my "PX privileges," the weekly time allotted for each soldier to visit the Base exchange (store). A written record of this event was given to me in a brown envelope that I was instructed to give to my unit supervisor however I lost it in transit from Ft. Benning, Georgia to Schofield Barracks, Hawaii.

My first army duty station was Schofield Barracks, Hawaii. I was 19 and happy to be there. When I arrived at my unit on the second floor, a fight had just ended between a black guy and a white guy — both easily over 200 pounds. The condition of the hallway suggested that this had happened a lot. There were multiple human-sized holes in the drywall that looked like someone had fallen into them.

As soon as I walked into my room and dropped my bags, I saw the white guy who'd been fighting earlier stop outside my door. "My name is Powell. Anytime you're looking for trouble, I live in room 200." Right after he leaves the black guy Powell had been fighting earlier stops outside of my door and says, "My name is Johnson. Anytime they want to throw down, I live in Room 210." I didn't say much of anything to either of them. I just kind of acknowledged with a nod and closed my door. Unbeknownst to them, a fight would have been just fine with me.

I was hanging around my unit late in the day when my first sergeant walked up and started talking to me. He asked me to take a walk with him and as we strolled through the barracks I told him jokes that made him laugh.

The next day at morning formation the first sergeant greeted the company by telling the jokes I had told him the day before. We all burst out laughing. This led to a special relationship between First Sergeant Fernandez and me. Since my last name is Richardson everybody ended up calling me Daddy Rich. However, the first sergeant called me Rick and watched out for me. In fact, if the First Sergeant Fernandez hadn't bailed me out of my many mistakes, I most likely would have been booted out of the army. Since leaving the army, I have tried to find him — many times without success — to see if he needed help with anything.

During my eight years in the military, I toured Australia, Panama, Germany, Japan and San Diego and communist East Berlin for one day when the company selected a couple dozen people to go. There was also a tour to Korea but I did not go because I was in school studying to get my General Education Diploma (GED) since I had dropped out of high school. Shortly thereafter, I took college courses on the base for two years.

I was a young man who had not yet learned how to avoid trouble and ended up getting into numerous confrontations — some very serious.

I recall one such incident where I got into a fight with a sergeant and they threatened to take a rank from me as a result. I was pulling guard duty at the time and doing four hours on and eight hours off for 24 hours with the next day off. I was into my sixth hour of off time and asleep in bed when the sergeant of the guard came to my room and told me I had to go back two hours earlier than was scheduled. I was unhappy about that and somehow fell back asleep. The sergeant came back to my room, knocked on the door and yelled, "If you are not downstairs and ready for guard in five minutes, I am going to kick your butt." I replied as I opened the door,

"If you think you are man enough to do it, then come and do it." He came back in and we fought briefly.

When I went downstairs I was written up through my battalion meaning I was in BIG TROUBLE. They were going to write me up for an Article 15, which is disciplinary action that could involve any number of consequences including some form of incarceration, docking pay, reducing rank, giving extra duties, and just about anything they could think of.

The next couple of days were very rough for me and my platoon non-commissioned officers (NCO) did anything and everything they could do to make me miserable while I awaited my punishment.

The first sergeant was on leave so I called to apprise him of my situation, hoping he could somehow help. I didn't get through. Though he was on leave, he was still on the island and one morning when he came to check on things, I told him what had happened and he shook his head and said, "Rick, if I was a private and a sergeant said that to me, I'd kick his butt too!"

As I mentioned before, he was like a father to me. Immediately after our talk he gathered the platoon NCOs to chew them out for messing with me. He was serious. I could hear him yelling at them from down the street! The first sergeant worked his magic and I avoided punishment. When he returned from vacation, I told him that the NCOs were still bothering me on the sly and that I wanted to transfer platoons. He asked me which one and I said I wanted to go to the Third Platoon and that was the end of that. He used to tell me, "Rick, anything you want is easy." I loved that man. If it weren't for him, I would have been kicked out of the army early on.

I was only 19 and though legally an adult, I was not yet a full grown man. One day I ran into a fellow soldier I had gone to basic training with and, since it was pay day, we ended up hanging out on base at the PX. We were trying on sunglasses when he got the idea to leave the store without paying. Now, I never stole at home but being stupid, I followed his example. As soon as we exited the store we were approached. I told him to just keep walking. By the time I got to my unit I was told the military police had been looking for me.

Again, it was First Sergeant Fernandez who handled this for me. I got off with a suspended Article 15 with mandatory extra duty for two weeks, which translated to cleaning offices for two hours after work every day.

Yes, at times I was a black spot on my platoon, but I also helped my platoon shine. One of the things my platoon really liked about me was that I was able to max out the army's Physical Training (PT) test, garnering recognition for the platoon. I could max the PT test even with no sleep and a hangover with 69 correct pushups (going down so low my chest nearly touched the floor), 69 correct sit-ups in two minutes, and run two miles in less than 12 minutes. Another big plus for me was that I would lead the whole platoon in PT AND I could get out there and call cadence during the two to three mile run at the end of PT for at least a mile, which most soldiers didn't have the stamina for.

The next time I got into trouble was about two years later when I was an E-4. I was assigned a room with Sergeant Billard, a black man from Memphis, Tennessee who spoke kind of funny. His missing front teeth caused him to lisp. When I first met him, he introduced himself as being from "Thol thitty," like I should know exactly where that was. But I didn't so I asked, "Where?"
"Thol thitty. You know Thol thitty!"

Someone passing by overheard us and told me, "Soul City is what he's trying to say." Every word that he spoke came out this way and not having any front teeth didn't help at all.

Billard and I got along well enough, but we shared one key. And that was a problem because half the time he would leave the room with the only key in hand and I'd end up getting locked out. And no matter how many times I talked to him, begging him to leave the key with the CQ (charge of quarters) desk, he'd forget. On a side note, for those of you unfamiliar with the military, the person tasked with CQ duty is sort of like the front desk clerk at a hotel. But really, he is tasked with guarding the front entrance of the barracks. Well, one night, I talked to him again about the key situation. He was apologetic about forgetting to leave the key with the CQ and promised to remember the next time.

Satisfied, I went outside to go to the showers. There were no showers in the rooms at the time and when I returned, Billard was gone. I went downstairs to check with the CQ hoping he'd left the key with him. He said that no key was left.

Here I stood with just a towel wrapped around my waist and flip flops on my feet. I was boiling! I stomped up the steps to the second floor, pushed out the ceiling tile as I'd done about a dozen times before, lifted myself up and onto the ceiling of my room, removed the ceiling tile from the inside of my room and jumped down inside. Needless to say, I lost the towel along the way. This was probably the angriest I had been in years. I'd had a hard day and now I wondered how he could possibly forget to leave the key when I had JUST asked him to remember to leave it at the CQ desk right before I'd left for my shower!

The casement windows were wide open and, in a fit, I grabbed both his TV and his stereo and threw them out the second story window.

It would be easy to say that he was doing it on purpose — I'd been locked out at least a dozen times before this — but aside from locking me out of the room, we didn't have any other issues. I settled down after my fit and eventually went to bed.

Early next morning, around 4 a.m., there was a knock at the door. I was told to go see the platoon sergeant about the incident. I was to get another Article 15 for chucking Billard's belongings out the window. Later that day when I saw the first sergeant, he told me that he had spoken to the commander and recommended a suspension, extra duty and that I repay the sergeant for his losses. This proved to me that guardian angels do exist and this would be the last time I would get into trouble of this magnitude.

Military personnel change duty stations approximately every two to three years. When the first sergeant got his orders to change duty stations, I almost cried. In the short time I'd come to know First Sergeant Fernandez he'd become a mentor and a father-figure to me. I was sure going to miss him.

Shortly after the first sergeant left, platoon Sergeant Pelupelu, my Samoan squad leader, sat me down to have a career talk. He asked me if I wanted to see younger guys coming into the army and supervising me. I said, "NO!" He told me then that I'd better start being a better soldier. So I did.

Back in the day, there weren't very many black Americans in the military — maybe only a handful in every platoon — and in my eyes, favoritism among the white community ran rampant. I frequently witnessed new recruits receiving a promotion before someone who'd been in longer. As far as I could tell, it was outright favoritism. I had come into the military already angry and being treated unfairly only served to stoke the fire within me. Up until that point, whenever I'd witnessed something unjust I would speak out and make waves. And I would do it loudly. But with Sergeant Pelupelu, who was not part of the good old boys club and who offered a chance to get promoted, I decided to silence my tongue and adjust my attitude.

I was sent a year later to Fort Riley, Kansas. Believe it or not, after only a few months there I ran into First Sergeant Fernandez! He was now a sergeant major. There were three other sergeant majors with him when we bumped into each other and I felt intimidated. However, he spoke to me as an equal as he introduced each one of them to me. I thanked him many times over for all he'd done for me on my road to maturity and becoming a man.

At Fort Riley I re-enlisted so I could return to Hawaii. My goal was to make the rank of sergeant. I studied, went before a board and passed the exam. I was scheduled to go to leadership school, which was intense training that lasted 30 days and nights — including weekends.

I packed my bags, moved into the school and immediately became friends with two other students who also happened to be comedians. We just could not stop laughing! The most embarrassing moment was when I was marching them along with several other troops. They were retelling an earlier joke — one which caused us all to fall on the ground laughing — when the instructor caught us and asked me, "Is that how you're going to handle your troops, Richardson? Laugh at them?" In spite of the rough start, I passed school on time and was promoted to an E-5, or sergeant.

About a year later, while still stationed in Hawaii, new recruits arrived. I was lucky enough to get one on my team. He was fresh out of high school. Little did I know that he would be crucial in helping me decide my future in the military.

That happened in the field one night. We had set up a perimeter with the entire platoon while the sergeants held a meeting near the center. I was in the middle of the meeting when the new recruit walked up to me and whispered that he was scared! I told him to get back to his position and that I'd be by to see him after the meeting. While I already had the feeling that there was something else out there for me, at the precise moment of our brief exchange I felt like a babysitter and decided to leave the army.

I was nearing the end of my second enlistment and everyone was sure I would re-enlist. I did not. Since I had acquired more than 45 days leave (vacation), I used it to exit the military 45 days prior to my ETS (end of time in service). My platoon gave me a very nice wooden plaque in the shape of a shield with fancy military trinkets and the inscription "Thank you for your service Sergeant Richardson."

Just prior to leaving the military I managed to buy a 1,200 square foot condo in Mililani using the Veteran's Administration's loan program. My time in the army helped shape me into a man. I was now a full grown man — a man who was ready to take on anything. Though I got into my fair share of trouble while enlisted, I also had a lot of good times in the U. S. Army.

A plate adorned with the town seal of Bayern, Germany

CHAPTER THREE

Heartwarming

My most memorable army experience was during a deployment called Northwind '87, when my platoon travelled in armored personnel carriers (APCs) while in Germany. Upon arrival, we were bussed to a large barn with fresh hay where we climbed into our sleeping bags to sleep for the night. We traveled in the APCs until a snowstorm the next day forced us to hold tight. The platoon lieutenant and first sergeant decided we would remain there until the weather improved.

We thought we were in the woods far from any urban area, but a short while later a group of neighborhood kids came over for a visit. We managed to convince the little boys, who were about 10 to 12 years old, to buy cigarettes and beer for us.

After a few hours passed the snow became a little slushy and the kids started throwing snowballs at us. Being soldiers, we had to retaliate. Quickly the snowballs became hard, almost rock-like. I don't know if the kids did it on purpose, but they were hitting some of the soldiers on the side of their head with these hard snowballs. Some of the angry soldiers chased down the kids and dusted them up. When I saw the kids' red faces, I switched sides. I decided to help the kids chase down some soldiers so the kids could get their revenge. It ended in good fun.

Later that day the kids showed up with their parents. All of the parents wanted to meet me to thank me for playing with and helping their kids. The kids brought us cakes spiked with rum and other alcohol. The kids' parents said that they wanted to give me their town seal. That spiked my curiosity and I asked to see it.

One of the fathers approached me and asked, "Are you Richardson?"
"Yes, I'm Richardson."
"We want to thank you for what you did to help our children," he said with a warm smile.
"Aww, it was nothing."
"Tomorrow we'll bring you our town seal. Okay?"
"Yeah sure. What is your town seal? What does it look like?" I asked curiously.

"When do you leave?" he asked.
"Tomorrow morning at 5 a.m."
"Okay, we will see you tomorrow morning," he said excitedly.
"Okay."

I didn't expect to see them again since we were leaving in the early morning, but as we were preparing our departure the platoon lieutenant walked up to me as I was loading my gear into the APC and said, "Richardson, there are some people here to see you." I walked down and saw the kids' parents walking toward me, each with boxes in their hands.

The boxes were gifts for me. The "town seal" they wanted to gift me turned out to be a full set of porcelain dishware that was decorated with the town seal. The set of dishware included coffee cups and saucers, dinner plates and soup bowls. They were beautiful. I thanked them profusely and exchanged hugs and shook hands. I found room for the four boxes on the APC.

Once I got the dishes back stateside, I sent them to my mother since I was living in the barracks and had no need for dishes. They are displayed in her china cabinet to this day.

CHAPTER FOUR

Sarah

After I left the army, I worked odd jobs until I found employment in the construction industry. Life was good. I was dating periodically and having fun. One particular relationship that stands out was with one of the prettiest black women I'd ever dated. Her name was Sarah.

It all started when I agreed to be the designated driver for two women I'd met at a party. They wanted to go to a club on the Marine Corps base in Kaneohe and since I wasn't a drinker I was perfect for the job. I agreed to accompany them because I wasn't doing anything else that night. We arrived at the club and scattered to check out the scene. I found a good spot to people watch and that's when I saw her. She was the prettiest girl in the club. She had light brown sugar-colored skin, a curvy and fit figure, gorgeous eyes, a beautiful smile and long black hair. She walked past me on her way to the ladies restroom. The two women I had accompanied popped up to chat, so I wasn't able to catch her when she left the restroom.

Once I stopped chatting with the two women, I walked around the entire club looking for her. I walked the club three times over and could find her nowhere. I parked myself in a corner and, sure enough, there she was smiling at me from across the room. I found out later that she had been amused watching me the entire time I was looking for her. I made a bee-line toward her and asked her to dance. She smiled at me coyly and said, "OK." We danced to four songs back to back, while talking and laughing. She told me her name was Sarah and that she had come to Hawaii as a traveling registered nurse to work at one of the local hospitals. Her friend, Annabelle, showed up when we got off the dance floor. Annabelle was in Hawaii by way of her husband who was serving in the U.S. Army. I told them the only reason why I was at the club that night was to be the designated driver for a couple of friends. Sarah and I really hit it off and we ended up exchanging numbers at the end of the night.

The next day I called Sarah and invited her to join me at one of the nicest restaurants on the island. The restaurant was on the top floor of the Waikiki Gateway Hotel. It had a breathtaking panoramic view and a coziness that could lull you to sleep. Dinner was a blur as we focused on getting to know each other. We stretched the evening out with glasses of wine after dinner, talking, laughing and discovering the intimate details of each other's lives. Neither of us had ever been married nor did we have any children. After that evening we started dating and talked daily on the phone. We had been dating for a couple of months when I disclosed to her that I had two round trip tickets to London that I'd bought at an auction a few years prior. I had already called the issuing company and extended the tickets for two years. Now the tickets had a one-year expiration date. Use them or lose them. The tickets were purchased during a prior relationship and when that relationship dissolved I had no one to take with me ... until now. So I asked Sarah if she'd be interested in traveling to London with me.

"You have round trip tickets to London?" she asked. Yes, I can go," she answered in a very cool non-excited tone.
"Have you ever traveled outside of the country?" I asked her.
"No."

I thought she was acting pretty cool after being asked to go on an all-expense paid vacation but I decided to let it slide.

"Okay, I'll make the flight reservations and find us a decent hotel."

So it was set. We were to travel together to London in a month's time. I made hotel reservations for us at a 4-star Holiday Inn in South Kensington.

Time flew by and the next thing we knew we were packed and excitedly heading to the airport for our trip to London. It was a long trip. We first flew from Hawaii to New York on a nonstop 8-hour flight and then from New York to Heathrow Airport in London. Though long, the trip was smooth and uneventful. We talked, ate and slept our way through the flight. When we arrived at the hotel, I have to say that if the name hadn't been hanging outside the hotel, I would have sworn we'd arrived at a Hilton or a Hyatt. The Holiday Inn had a well-appointed lobby and the room was exceptional, with a king-sized bed, porcelain tub/shower and a beautiful view of a park.

Sarah and I were so excited that we could hardly wait to hit the town and try some restaurants! The size of most restaurants surprised me; they were small to say the least! It was 1992 and many of the restaurants we passed could barely fit seven tables. However, size was clearly not a good indicator of food quality because in spite of their minute square footage the food never failed to impress us. Every restaurant's food tasted like it was prepared by a 5-star establishment. And that was true of the food in the Holiday Inn as well. The hotel advertised Curry Night the following evening and boasted six different types of Indian curries to choose from. We sampled all six and they were some of the best curries I've ever had to date.

We explored London and Paris, hitting up all the tourist spots. In London we took a double-decker bus tour and bought tickets to a popular musical called 5 Guys Named Moe at London's West End. I gave it 4.5 stars. Our London shopping experience is probably unmatched anywhere else in the world with the endless array of shops in a very clean city. In Paris we visited the Eiffel Tower and we took a train to visit Versailles. It was the trip of a lifetime.

During our trip I started to notice that Sarah had become a bit argumentative about almost everything, from restaurant choices to day trips. I did my best to stay upbeat and have a good vacation rather than fanning the flames of discontent.

When we returned to London on our final night we ate at the Elephant on the River (later renamed Elephant and Castle). The restaurant's food and service was the best we'd experienced on the entire trip. It has left me with fond memories. And with that dinner our 5-day vacation to Europe came to a very satisfying end.

Sarah and I continued to date over the next several months and it was very good. About six months after she told me her contract with the hospital was about to expire and that she would need to find another nursing job elsewhere in the city. The expiration of her work contract also meant she'd have to find a new place to live because the hospital paid for her lodging as part of the contract. Logically, I invited her to move in with me. Being young and inexperienced, I told her she wouldn't need to help with the rent. Sarah accepted and happily moved in with me.

Sarah started working night shifts after her contracted ended while I worked from 7 a.m. to 3:30 p.m., usually getting home around 4:30 p.m. Her work schedule occasionally included weekends and holidays.

In spite of our conflicting schedules we were still able to carve out date nights. I recall one night when we had a double date with Sarah's co-worker Annabelle and her husband. We attended a jazz concert in the ballroom of a new hotel. We sat at one end of a long table with the women between us. Sarah and Annabelle were busily chatting away with each other when three older black women came and sat in the chairs next to me. When I say older, I mean old enough to be my mom. Since I wasn't being included in Sarah and Annabelle's conversation, I struck up a conversation with the older woman next to me. We started with small talk; I told her I was a construction worker and she told me she was the president of the Hawaii chapter of the NAACP. The conversation got busy after that introduction. Suddenly, without so much as looking at me or saying one word to me, Sarah gracefully rose from our table and sat at another table nearby and started making conversation with some guy. I'm not the kind of man who likes to make a scene, so I got up and walked over to tell Sarah I was leaving. Sarah arrived at the car about a minute after I did.

"You want to tell me what that was all about?" I asked her.
"If you can talk to other women I can talk to other men."
"Oh my God, you're jealous?!" I was incredulous. "First of all, she's old enough to be my mother!" (I was 29 at the time.)
Sarah started to rant and eventually said, "I want to know just who she is!"
"She's the president of the NAACP."
"Well, I don't care who she thinks she is!"

She ranted all the way home. I was in shock. I could not believe what was happening and how jealous Sarah was. As if things weren't bad enough already, as we stepped through the front door the phone rang. Sarah picked it up and immediately stormed into the bathroom and locked the door. She had never done that before.

I stood outside the bathroom door and strained to listen in on the conversation. When Sarah came out I asked her who she had been talking to and why she needed to take the conversation behind a locked bathroom door. "Nobody important," she replied flippantly. I was infuriated by her actions and manner. I grabbed her by both shoulders and shook her, telling her to stop lying. "Well, if you can talk to other women, I can talk to other men!" she yelled.

It was a weeknight and it had gotten late. I was used to waking at 5 a.m.

for work so I left it at that, showered and went to bed. When I left for work the following morning Sarah was still in bed. When I returned home that afternoon, Sarah was walking around with sunglasses on. I asked, "Why are you wearing dark sunglasses in the house?" She ignored me. I asked again and she took off the sunglasses long enough for me to see she was sporting a black eye. "How did you get that black eye?" She was silent. No reply. She just glared at me.

It was at this point that I felt I had to call my sister, Lori, for advice and tell her what had happened. Lori told me I shouldn't be putting up with a woman who was as ungrateful as Sarah and under no circumstance should I put my hands on her while angry because she could be goading me to get me locked up. I told her that I had never hit Sarah or any other woman and that I didn't know how she got the black eye.

"How do you know she's really got a black eye? Maybe she's faking it."
"I don't know. It looks pretty real to me. All I know is that I never hit her. When I left her this morning her face was just fine. I don't hit women."
"Well, just be careful of what you do with her from now on."
"Thanks, Lori. I really appreciate the advice. Talk to you later. I love you."
"Call anytime. I love you too."

Afterward I told Sarah that the next time we have a situation like this we'll call it quits and go our separate ways.

During our time together I'd been working on becoming a licensed contractor. One day I was outside on the front balcony talking to some construction guys who lived next door. They worked for a company based in Arizona that had a contract to build a housing complex nearby. They knew I was in construction too so they asked if I had a SKIL saw because they needed a piece of plywood cut. I did and made the 8-foot long cut for them. I headed back into the house after and Sarah, who had the day off, was impressed with my skills. She told me that she liked my display of physical prowess. I told her I was working on getting a contractor's license and she suddenly changed up on me.

"Wait a minute. We don't need two professional licenses in one house."
"Say what?" I responded, surprised.
"One professional license is all that's needed."
"I'm going to be a contractor whether you like it or not." We said not one more word. We never broached the subject again. I like keeping the peace

and I figured any more talking wasn't going to change things.

Sarah was a very attractive black woman. Her skin was a shade lighter than mine. She was smart, articulate and had a beautiful, trim body. My concern now was where our relationship was going. I wanted to start a family since neither of us had children so I initiated a conversation to that end.

"Hey, Sarah, I'm going to buy life insurance. It'll be enough to cover burial expenses and pay off the condo just in case something happens to me. I've been thinking about making you my beneficiary. Is that OK with you?"
"Yeah, that's OK."
"I know you have a life insurance policy too. Are you going make me your beneficiary?"
She looked down and didn't respond.
Maybe she didn't hear me correctly? "If I make you my beneficiary are you going to make me yours?" Who's your current beneficiary in the event you die because you're living here with me?"
"Well ... I have a son."

I was completely unprepared for that response.

"I'm sorry. My ex is a Memphis police officer. When I got pregnant he promised me that we'd be a family but what I didn't know was that at the same time, he'd gotten another woman across town pregnant. After our son was born he wouldn't help with the child support or anything."
"Oh my God" I was floored. "Where's the baby now?"
"He's with his dad. He promised to help out and when he wouldn't I decided to move away to another state. We agreed that he should watch our son for a couple of months while I went to research Atlanta and other cities for job opportunities and housing. But when I returned to Memphis I found out that not only did my ex pull a fast one on me and got full custody from the court, but now I have to pay him monthly child support."

This confession was like having a hydrogen bomb dropped on me. It explained a lot. It explained why Sarah was so ungrateful though she was living here rent free and bill free and never once offered to pay for anything.

"Sarah, do you remember our first date when both of us said that neither

one of us had any children?"
"Antonio, I'm sorry but I was afraid if I told you that I had a child so early on that it might scare you away."
"Now I understand. I feel like no matter what I do I'm not appreciated. No matter how much I do for you it's never enough."
Sarah was silent.
"Is there anything else you haven't told me?"
"No," she replied quietly.

Early November that same year Sarah started to complain that the long-distance provider was over-charging her. I told her to ask for a refund. A few days later she told me that they would only speak with me about the account since it was in my name. I suggested that she activate and use the second phone line that ran into the apartment. I told her that there was an independent phone jack in the spare bedroom so whenever I rented out that room the tenant would have their own phone line. She thought it was a great idea and within a few days it was in operation.

Sarah and I still worked conflicting schedules. About a week after the phone line was activated in the spare bedroom the phone rang while she was at work. Thinking it was a long distance call, I picked up and to my surprise it was a guy asking for Sarah. "Sarah's not here. Would you like to leave a message?" The caller said, "No," and hung up.

I watched this activity for a little while to see where it went. I never told Sarah about the phone call and apparently the caller didn't either, because he continued to call for a couple more weeks. A week before Thanksgiving our next door neighbor came over to plan a dinner with us. We were lounging on the sofa when Sarah's phone started ringing. She excused herself to answer it. I excused myself a second later and walked down the hallway after her, stopping just outside the spare bedroom door where Sarah couldn't see me. I heard her say, "I don't have a boy-friend. I have a roommate." That was all I needed to hear before making my decision. I walked into the room and ripped the phone cord out of the wall.

"You don't have a roommate! Remember that discussion we had when I told you that if this scenario ever happened again, we were done? GET OUT!" I was furious and so disappointed.
She yelled at me, "NO!"
"I'll give you an hour to pack up all your stuff," and I walked out.

I waited on the couch in the living room thinking I knew this day was going to come and now that it was here, I couldn't wait to get her out of my life. While she should have been packing she just sat around and kept saying she wasn't going to leave. After her hour was up, I picked her up physically and carried her down the hallway. She fought the whole way, grabbing onto the corners of walls but I prevailed. I got her outside and put her down gently, closed the door and locked it.

Ten minutes later there was a knock at the door. It was a couple of police officers. They told me that I had to let Sarah in to retrieve her belongings. I held the door wide open and told the officers that I had asked her several times to get her things and leave and she refused. It had been her choice. Sarah sulked in the background and at the officers' urgings she entered and started gathering her belongings. The policemen and I sat at opposite ends of the sofa and watched her. Twenty minutes later, she was out the door with everything. It was over. I was relieved. I closed the door after the officers stepped out and locked it. She was gone.

The following day I felt as if a ton of weight had been lifted off my shoulders. I found out weeks later that Sarah had moved in temporarily with her friend and co-worker, Annabelle. I half expected to see her in the clubs around town on the weekend but I never did.

I did, however, run into Sarah while checking on jobs my company had completed in the Aikahi Park Shopping Center about two years later. I was walking to my truck when I spotted her in the parking lot. We exchanged hellos and she seemed genuinely excited to see me. She told me that she lived on the Windward side of the island, only minutes away from where we were standing. She wanted me to see her home and encouraged me to follow her there. I did. She lived in a separate portion of a single family home with her own private entrance. It was a nice place. Sarah apologized for the bad behavior she exhibited that prompted me to throw her out. She told me that her son was coming to town for a couple of weeks and wanted me to meet him. I agreed.

When Sarah's son, Jason, arrived, she called to let me know and asked if I could spend a day with him while she was busy working. Sarah and I met up at the same shopping center where we'd bumped into each other. Jason climbed into my truck and off we went to cruise around the island. We drove all over before returning to my apartment in Mililani to take a swim. It was at the pool where Jason asked me to marry his mom.

Immediately, I thought she'd put that idea into his head. I simply told him, "I really wanted to marry your mommy but she's too crazy for me." We stayed at the pool until the sun got too hot and then went for another drive. He was very interested in driving, so I told him I'd give him a driving lesson only if he agreed to do exactly as I told him while he had the steering wheel. He eagerly agreed. There was a technology park just up the hill from my place where there was very little traffic. I gave him a 10-minute driving lesson just for fun. He had a blast and grinned from ear to ear the whole time.

Sarah came by after work and picked up her son from my place. We said our goodbyes and that was the last time I ever saw Sarah. However, she did contact me by phone many times even after she moved back stateside. Eventually she stopped calling.

In my opinion, the main problem I had with Sarah was that she had not fully recovered from her past relationship with her ex-boyfriend and was not ready for a serious relationship when we'd met. I received a lot of anger and resentment that was totally misdirected. Otherwise, if things had been different, I most likely would have married her. I sure wanted to.

After Sarah, I thought to myself, "You know, I really don't deserve this. I live in Hawaii and I limit myself to dating only black women. I should be enjoying the company of any woman that I'm interested in if she's interested in me. I am no longer going to limit myself to one ethnicity. I will date whomever I like.

CHAPTER FIVE

Construction

In 1990, well before I had met Sarah, I decided to rent out the spare bedroom to help with the mortgage payments. My first tenant was an older man from Fairbanks, Alaska. He was one of many carpenters who had heard of the extremely high wages Hawaii paid on government construction jobs. I showed him the place and told him to just clean up after himself and all would be good. At the time I worked two jobs and every day when I came home, he would always ask me, "How did they treat you today?"

One day he asked me if I would like to have a construction job. He explained what was required and I decided to give it a go. The pay for a laborer was $25 an hour for government work. We worked well together until he suddenly quit his job and returned home to Alaska due to a family emergency. I was promoted shortly after from laborer to heavy forklift operator which paid $30 an hour. My boss was a tough guy who did not really care for me but totally respected my work ethic. By the middle of the third year, he sometimes would consult with me about specific aspects of jobs. I had won him over.

At my next construction job I met the contractor who taught me the necessary skills to start up my own company. While working on the forklift one day, he stopped me to ask if I had a room for rent. I told him I did, so he followed me home after work to check it out. He liked my place and decided to take it. The next morning he asked me if I was interested in helping him at work. He said he was installing all the windows and glass doors for all of the three buildings we were constructing. I told him to ask my boss and if he agreed, I would do it. Luckily my boss was fine with it so we worked together on and off for the following 18 months. Sometimes he returned to the mainland for a couple of months while waiting for window and door openings to be completed.

The project as a whole won a local building award. It was completed in the middle of 1992 and for the first time since 1989 I found myself without work. However, when my boss encouraged me to obtain my contractor's license, at 29 years of age I filed for unemployment insurance for the first time in my adult life. I attended contractor's licensing school where I studied old tests and books pertaining to glaziers, my industry classification. After three months I passed the state exam for the C-22 Glazier's license. The licensing board informed me that I would need a $15,000 bond before being able to move forward.

I was broke at the time and the bonding insurance company wanted half in cash. I hustled to raise the money and began to sell some household items. Among those things was a brand new piano that I was hoping to learn to play for $3,000. I also enclosed two of my neighbors' lanais with windows for $2,500 each, to come up with the remainder I needed to secure the bond. I was off to what I thought was a solid start as a contractor. The next thing I did was buy the computer my neighbor was selling along with his dot matrix printer. With the help of a local contracting agency I found local, state and federal construction projects to bid on in addition to some private projects.

Luck was with me when a few months later a local development corporation (LDC) was sponsoring a project to help small businesses acquire small loans. The maximum amount one could borrow was $50,000. I thought that this would be just enough to get me out of my condo bedroom and into a shop with some money remaining for other business expenses. I started visiting the LDC classes and talked to their staff about applying for the maximum loan. I was told I'd need to create a business plan, supply two years of tax returns and have a good credit rating. My bookkeeper helped me to create a three-year income projection and I took out a second mortgage on my condo to secure the loan. I was informed that I was the first one in the state to get a loan approved. I was featured in the 1993 issue of Pacific Business News, photo and all. And so I began my career as a glass contractor.

I used the loan to open a shop and buy a new truck, work tools and some inventory. Things were slow until I got a listing in the phone book a few months later. I specialized in glass, mirror and window supplies and installation. I found working in the office to be completely different from working in the field.

Almost everything I did in the early days was based on trial and error. I felt a lot better once I got help from a friend's father who was already working as an estimator and fabricator in a window shop. I quickly realized that this type of work takes time to learn; it is something you grow into. And grow it did albeit slowly. At one point I had projects on Oahu as well as three outer islands and I was short on skilled labor. Against my better judgment I joined the Glazier's union as a conduit for skilled labor. Unfortunately, the quality of skilled labor varied.

In one instance there was a six-figure project on a neighboring island that ran into a snag. The general contractor called to inform me that I needed to get replacements for three union workers I'd sent because they had materials scattered across the work site while they stood around for two days scratching their heads.

In the following year there was another incident that could have become a major snafu. On a federal contract project, again in the six-figure range, I again hired union workers. After losing an argument with the general contractor over who was going to provide the required backing for my windows — a detail the general contractor missed — I was forced to unexpectedly provide extra materials and labor. The union representative suggested that I pay the workers cash. I told him, "No, I can't do that. It's a federal contract!" Two weeks later I was audited by the general contractor. I was being accused of paying the extra union hires cash on a federal construction project. My first response was, "Absolutely not!" I provided copies of the certified payroll and the payroll checks along with check stubs for the temporary hires. The matter was quickly resolved but I was furious. This was an obvious attempt to not only throw me off the project, but to ban me indefinitely from other federal projects.

Three years had passed since I opened the business. The mistakes I had made were costly and I saw no way to move forward. I filed Chapter 7 bankruptcy to get a fresh start and end my contract with the union. Business was fine thereafter and my business was as busy as I wanted it to be.

My social life was alright as well. I had a girlfriend every now and then and I had the freedom to decide at the beginning of the week where I wanted to travel to the coming weekend. Life was good and I was pretty wild for a short time until I met my wife. Masako was from Japan and she was attending a local business college. When we started dating in 2001 I started to vomit almost regularly for seemingly no reason. Much later my nephrologist told me that acid reflux disease was causing the vomiting.

Surfacing Health Issues

About 14 months after we started dating, Masako and I got married. I applied for life insurance and a few months later a nurse came to our house to draw blood and collect a urine sample. I gave her a check and that was that. Everything seemed fine until one month later when I received a letter from the life insurance company stating, "We're sorry but we can't insure you. Please find a copy of your lab results and a check enclosed for the return payment. Take the lab results to your doctor immediately." The letter gave no diagnosis and no reason for rejecting my application. This was the first indication that there was something awry with my health. Both my wife and I were a bit concerned but neither of us suspected that it was anything serious.

I brought the lab results to my doctor, Joseph Robertson, the very next day — February 12th, my birthday. He ran the same tests the insurance company had performed and told me that I had high blood pressure and high cholesterol. That day he started me on medication to control both. I went home feeling that I had addressed my health issues and that everything was fine. I had absolute faith in my doctor. After all, not only did we have a good understanding as doctor and patient (so I thought) but I had also done some construction work for him.

I continued working as a contractor and did my best to keep my doctor's appointments to maintain my health though I rescheduled missed appointments occasionally. About the same time, I started experiencing erectile dysfunction as a result of my now high blood pressure, though I was unaware of the cause at the time. Masako really wanted to start a family, but it just wasn't happening. Hoping to find a solution to my difficulty performing in bed, I convinced Masako to watch pornography with me. My new wife indulged the idea once or twice but in the end she opted out, so I trashed the idea. Month after month we tried but we couldn't conceive. We decided to go to a children's hospital to get ourselves checked. After reviewing the test results, the doctors determined that there was nothing wrong with Masako. Her menstrual cycles were regular and everything seemed fine. They could find no reason why she couldn't get pregnant. I, on the other hand, was a completely different story. I was told that I had a low sperm count. This came as a complete shock to me and eventually led to our divorce later that year. She couldn't accept adoption as a viable alternative.

Although I continued to take the blood pressure medication it did absolutely nothing to lower my blood pressure. Eventually one of my medications started to make me so nauseous that I'd vomit. I reported my vomiting episodes to Dr. Robertson, and he prescribed Phenergan. Phenergan triggered deep sleep episodes but did work a little to improve my nausea and vomiting.

I worked long hours as a contractor. Being a contractor was highly stressful, especially since I was the estimator, project manager and general manager all in one. My blood pressure roamed in the 160/110 range with the medications my primary care physician (PCP) prescribed.

Three months later in December 2003, about two years after I went to my PCP following the rejection notice from the insurance company, I got a very bad toothache. I went to see a dentist who determined that a root canal was needed to repair a bad cavity. The dentist performed the root canal but at the end of the procedure he told me that I would need to come back since he was unable to extract the entire tooth. I was shocked. Two weeks later I returned to have the extraction completed. That's when I discovered that the dentists in this clinic rotated. There were several clinics and getting the same dentist required proper scheduling. Not knowing any better and in a little pain, I let the new dentist complete the root canal. He proceeded with a very painful numbing and removal process that was the most pain I'd ever experienced. He could not remove the rest of the tooth because the unusually long root was difficult to access. I was in severe pain at the end of the appointment and I needed help NOW. I left the clinic and walked into the first dental office I saw. Dr. Staphe Fujimoto was Japanese and he was very skilled. I told him everything that had happened at the other clinic and he agreed to help me right away. With the help of his assistant the remainder of my root canal procedure was almost painless. I was so grateful that I thanked him over and over. Dr. Fujimoto remains my dentist to this day.

It was unknown to me then that with a glomerular filtration rate (GFR)[2] of 20 or less, a bad cold, a tooth infection or any type of traumatic event to the body can send the kidneys to stage 5 end stage kidney disease requiring immediate dialysis (according to my nephrologist). I discovered later that this root canal fiasco had pushed me into Stage 5 Chronic Kidney Disease.

---

2 A GFR test estimates kidney efficiency.

PART II

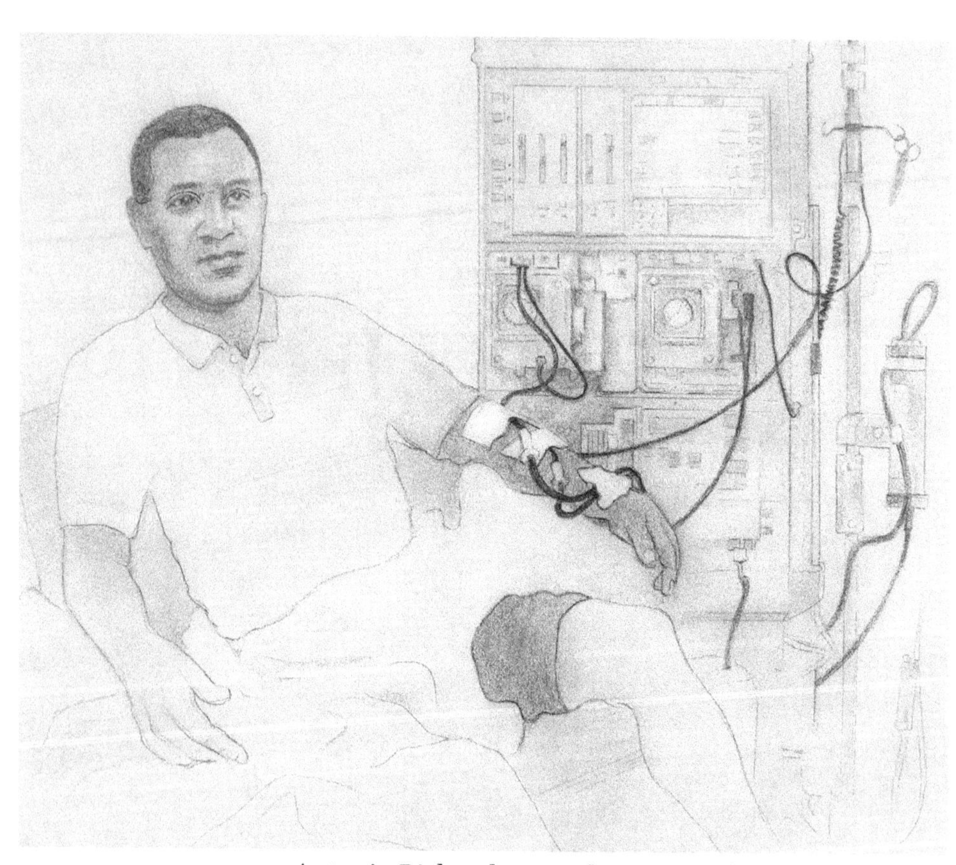

Antonio Richardson undergoing a dialysis treatment.

CHAPTER SIX

Dialysis

On June 9, 2004, I made my first visit to Dr. Fumi Horita, a nephrologist. On first impression, she looked as though she was about my age, attractive and very knowledgeable. We started my visit with questions about my family and a medical history before proceeding with a complete examination and a 24-hour urine test.

Since my primary care physician Dr. Robertson had not resolved the problem of my high blood pressure in the two-and-a-half years that I had seen him, she assumed that responsibility as well. She changed all my blood pressure medications.

When my medical exam was done our conversation flowed naturally to other subjects. As I readied to leave, she drew me back in to sit for another discussion. This sequence repeated itself a few times before I finally left. I was scheduled for a follow-up visit to see her about the lab work two days later and I could hardly wait for that day to come. I felt I was in very good hands with Dr. Horita and our conversation left me feeling invigorated.

The days passed quickly and during my follow up visit with Dr. Horita, she informed me that I needed immediate dialysis. She expressed her surprise at my ability to remain standing considering the seriousness of my lab results. My kidneys, under the care of my previous PCP, had apparently deteriorated to the point of not functioning. In addition, my potassium level was super high — around 7.8 — vs. a normal healthy person's 5.0 or lower. Dr. Horita, realizing this, told me that she was shocked that I was still standing. She explained that having a potassium level that high could easily stop a person's heart. I was shocked. She had made an appointment with a vascular surgeon for the following day. There was no time to waste. A catheter was installed through a jugular vein on the side of my neck since there were no prior preparations for a fistula.[3]

---

3   Use of a fistula is the desired method for hemodialysis (HD), a procedure that filters blood outside the body. A fistula, or a graft, is a connection between an artery and a vein that allows rapid blood flow through the vein. A dialysis catheter is a plastic tube with one opening residing outside the body and the opposite end sitting in the body and stopping just before the heart.

A positive aspect of having a dialysis catheter is that in an emergency a person needing immediate dialysis can be administered to within 24 to 48 hours, easily saving a life. However, there are the many downsides. I encountered one of these drawbacks when the vascular surgeon administered too little numbing cream to my neck prior to cutting into me to install the catheter. It was by far the most excruciating pain I'd ever experienced in my life. I laid there screaming and squeezing the nurse's hand. The doctor never stopped even though I was screaming. Nor did he ask if I wanted additional numbing as if it this suffering were normal. I found out later that doctors are supposed to stop and correct the situation when they are notified of pain during the procedure. However, it seems that experiencing such pain during that procedure isn't unusual. I've talked with several nurses who have witnessed similar horrifying experiences with other patients.

Another potential problem with using a catheter is how effectively (or not) it can clean your blood. Dialysis clinics have a protocol that mandates all patients' blood be cleaned at a minimum of 70 percent. My blood was only effectively cleaned to a maximum of 60-65 percent. Consequently, I often felt so nauseated that I'd vomit and just generally feel lousy for the rest of the day.

The worst drawback of having a dialysis catheter is that it can and often does get infected. It can be said that it's not a question of *if* it will get infected but *when*. An infected catheter can be deadly. My catheter got infected after only one month of use.

During my first month on dialysis, I informed Dr. Horita that I was considering a trip to Las Vegas. With the stress of work and all the craziness I experienced a few months earlier, I felt I needed to take a break. I bought tickets in anticipation of a much needed vacation. Dr. Horita was surprised that I would take a trip so soon after starting dialysis, but I wasn't expecting to have any problems. I was so naïve about the seriousness of my disease.

While in Las Vegas my legs swelled from excessive water retention. It was an uncomfortable feeling that I wasn't used to. My blood pressure rose and wouldn't come down until after my dialysis session the next day. I was having a good time in Vegas. Consuming too many liquids caused swelling in my legs, hands and feet. My body couldn't eliminate the extra fluids on its own, so I decided to cut my trip short and return home.

That was definitely a lesson learned.

I got my first catheter infection shortly after I returned to Hawaii. When I say infection, I don't mean a common skin infection that any person with a healthy immune system doesn't think twice about. I mean a blood infection that can kill a person within weeks. While on dialysis, a couple weeks after I returned home, I began to shiver under my blanket. Dialysis units are always cold and it's common for patients to be covered, but on that day I had a fever and chills. I asked the attending nurse to report what I was feeling. She immediately called Dr. Horita, who instructed the nurse to draw blood and have it tested. Having a fever while on dialysis usually indicates the beginning of an infection, but a blood test is required for confirmation. As soon as I completed my dialysis session I was taken to the hospital. The blood test confirmed that I had a serious blood infection and unbeknown to me at the time, it could have taken my life.

Dr. Fumi Horita Explains My Catheter Infection

Hemodialysis (HD) catheters remain in the body until a permanent access has been created and is ready for use. The inner portion of the HD catheter sits in the bloodstream and the outer portion sticks out of the skin. This allows a constant connection between the outside world and the sterile bloodstream. Bacteria can enter the blood through the catheter and result in a dangerous and even deadly bloodstream infection. Doctors don't allow patients to shower or get the catheter wet because bacteria can enter the body more easily between the catheter and the skin if wet. So if you know you're at high risk for kidney failure, you can plan ahead and schedule timely access to create a fistula through surgery to avoid any infections that are often caused by HD catheters.

Antonio didn't have the opportunity to plan ahead; he needed dialysis the week he met me. A bloodstream infection developed within a month of his HD catheter being placed in his body. He had a fistula surgically created shortly after starting dialysis, but fistulas can take months or more than a year to "mature" before use. His fistula took six months to mature. Meanwhile, HD was performed through the dialysis catheter placed into his jugular vein near his neck.

When he developed a fever and shaking chills during one of his treatments, his dialysis nurse called me to get orders for blood work and blood cultures. The results indicated a bloodstream infection, so we initiated antibiotics directly injected into his dialysis tubing into his bloodstream. These antibiotics are potent bacteria killers, but because the dialysis catheter is made of plastic, which is a nice home for bacteria, the antibiotic wasn't able to kill all the bacteria and his fever persisted. We needed to take the infected catheter out after his dialysis one Friday, leave the antibiotic circulating in his body over the weekend, then replace his infected catheter with a sterile one for dialysis the following Monday. That worked to eliminate the fever.

The blood cultures showed that Antonio had Methicillin Resistant Staphylococcus Aureus (MRSA) in his blood. This bacteria is especially resistant to first-line antibiotics and required vancomycin, a potent antibiotic, administered into his blood at the end of every dialysis treatment for six weeks. Bloodstream infections can cause low blood pressure, the need for hospitalization, and sometimes artificial blood pressure support. It can be deadly.

Antonio was fortunate that he was young, his heart was strong and he was physically fit enough to survive the MRSA bloodstream infection without having any of these dangerous outcomes. Were he elderly, frail, poorly nourished or living with a weak heart, he may not have survived the experience.

When we stopped the vancomycin after the six-week course was finished, during his next dialysis treatment his temperature spiked. His blood cultures showed the persistent presence of MRSA. The plastic catheter in his bloodstream continued to provide a home for MRSA. We completed a second six-week course of vancomycin and yet again his temperature spiked during his subsequent dialysis session. MRSA was cultured again from his blood because of his catheter. His surgeon was unwilling to allow us to try to use his fistula at that time because he did not feel it was mature. I decided to leave him on intravenous vancomycin with every dialysis until we could use his fistula and remove the catheter. After six months of dialysis, Antonio was finally catheter free and infection free. In addition, he was finally able to take a shower. After using his fistula, with the improved blood flow allowing better cleaning of his blood, freedom from the plastic catheter and the chronic inflammation caused by the catheter and MRSA, Antonio steadily began to feel better and regain strength. That was a cause for celebration.

Using a fistula felt like a huge reward compared to the catheter. With a fistula I could take showers, the dialysis machine could clean my blood better, and the best thing was no more catheter infections!

To me the biggest downside to using a fistula is feeling the needle poke into my vein. There is also the possibility of my spending a day in the hospital every 15 months or so to reopen a collapsed vein due to repetitive needle pokes. Still, overall it is vast improvement to having a catheter.

Surviving while on dialysis can be challenging. My first dialysis station was at a hospital before I was transferred two weeks later to a unit closer to my home. Along with the change of location came a change in schedule which was very difficult for me. I was placed on the night shift from 5 p.m. to 9 p.m. It became a real drag on my night life. On some Fridays I asked to be taken off the machine an hour earlier to go home, shower, and hit the clubs. This went on for a little while until my next doctor's visit with Dr. Horita, when she bluntly said, "So, you've been cutting your dialysis time." I surprisingly asked, "How do you know?" "We know everything," she replied. "When you shorten your dialysis, you shorten your time in that body." After that conversation, I never again cut short my time for the remaining seven years I was on dialysis.

I was in denial about having kidney failure well into my first year of treatment, especially since I was still able to urinate. However, my delusion ended after the first year on dialysis. The realization of my condition slowly set in as I compared my health and health challenges to that of other dialysis patients. Toward the end of that year my body stopped producing urine. Once you stop urinating a real challenge sets in. From the day I stopped urinating, I learned that any liquids that enter the body can only come out of the body by vomiting, diarrhea and a little through sweat, and dialysis. As a result, I had to restrict the amount of water I drank daily. The restrictions also extended to the foods I ate. I had to watch my potassium intake, water intake, salt intake — the list goes on.[4] My body would only allow the dialysis machine to remove three kilos of water per visit. If I dared to stay longer to remove more water, I would almost surely get a visit from a low-blood-pressure cramp. Imagine your worst cramp ever and then multiply it by three to get an idea of the amount of pain it can induce.

---

4   For details on how to best take care of oneself while on dialysis and thrive, here is a detailed personal account. Antonio Richardson , *Dialysis Your Way* (Honolulu, Kindle Direct Publishing, 2017).

Coping

The hemodialysis experience was an education in itself. Through the years I was on dialysis, I learned how to live as pain free as possible and how to best avoid the pitfalls that many dialysis patients experience. Things like feeling "wiped out" (extreme exhaustion), debilitating cramping, low blood pressure and life-threatening infections — all these and more I managed to navigate and come out on top. I did this by being mindful of my diet; establishing an exercise regimen; attending more consciously to my hygiene; taking my medication regularly and on time; and learning how to monitor my own stats during my dialysis sessions. I'm living proof that thriving as a dialysis patient can be done and done well.

Gradually, a friendship between the doctor and I developed. Under her care, working through the many struggles and challenges involved with my rocky transition to kidney failure, I began to look forward to my appointments. Sometimes, when I was her last patient for the day, we would talk about life after the medical stuff. After a few months, once I was medically more stable, I asked her to lunch. At first, she graciously declined, but eventually with my optimistic persistence, she agreed. We had a great time, talking about all kinds of things, and it was the beginning of a friendship in addition to the working doctor/patient relationship we already had.

However, it wasn't a friendship without challenges. One issue between us was the lawsuit. When I explained my plan to sue my primary doctor, she wanted nothing to do with it. She explained that probably all doctors dread the thought of being presented with a malpractice lawsuit. "We're human, we can make mistakes even though we are trying our very best to help our patients." The lawsuit seemed to create a riff in our friendship, and I wrestled with myself given the possible ramifications for weeks. During that time, we both did some soul searching. She eventually concluded that she would respect my decision on this. She said that once she was able to put aside her reactive fear of the word "lawsuit", she recognized the purpose for malpractice insurance. It was to help alleviate some of the associated economic burdens incurred from a doctor's mistake. If she made a mistake, she would want that money to be used to ease the pain, while realizing that money could never begin to right the wrong, or fix the damage done. With her newly found insight, I felt free to pursue my plan, without any toll on our friendship, as long as I didn't involve her. So, I worked on the lawsuit separate from our friendship.

Another challenge was her feelings against being a doctor for her friends and family. She felt it might compromise the quality of care she could deliver. It was a sad day when she asked me to seek another nephrologist of record, if we were to continue being friends. I didn't agree at first and tried to convince her otherwise, but I eventually saw her point. She was a strong doctor, but one with a soft, wimpy heart. If she was too emotionally connected, she worried that she wouldn't be able to make the right decisions, especially during times of medical crisis. She was afraid that if there was an unwanted outcome or death, which sometimes is inevitable, she might blame herself. She pointed out that she wanted to be a helpful, knowing daughter, mother, friend, and not a doctor for her parents, her son, or close friends. It was bittersweet that I now fell into the latter category. Reluctantly, I left her professional care in order to keep her friendship. It was a good decision because though it was not possible to duplicate her flavor as a treating nephrologist, I had her fully behind me with her heart and expertise as support.

Goody Two Shoes was my nickname for her. She grew up in a totally different environment from me. Her parents were devoted to, and very protective of her and her brother. They worked to provide for their children's advanced education, well into adulthood as they both attended medical school. She emerged as someone who always tried to do right, be fair, respect and trust everyone, and help others — including animals, plants, insects (though she kills cockroaches and ants in her house), the Earth and universe. I had to help her understand that not everyone is on your team in life. It is what it is. I have street smarts. I had lived through adversity, suffered from inequality, and while I keep a very positive outlook on where I'm going, I know who I can and cannot trust. She had no clue — naïve about a lot of things — and seemed to blindly trust everyone she met. That led to her being used and feeling hurt at times. I was able to help her see some situations from a different perspective.

Neither of us wanted false assumptions made about our friendship, which would likely foster rumors. It became our best kept secret even after I switched to another nephrologist's care. We were always patient and doctor in the dialysis unit or in and around the medical environment. Outside of the medical environment, she became my support system. She acted as my caregiver when times became dicey, like when I became very weak from a bloodstream infection or caught a bad virus that caused low blood pressure, or during the months of combination treatment with dialysis and chemotherapy. Because my family was in Mississippi, she became my family here. She was my only source of home cooked meals. When I had to give up my business and depend on a very limited Social Security check, she loaned me money when I came up short on rent. She provided emotional support, knowing I could depend on her to listen when I had questions or felt lost. She was someone I could cry with when the news of my myeloma seemed to nix my chances for a kidney transplant. She flew up to Chicago to be there for me after transplantation when I was most vulnerable after being discharged the first postoperative day. She went through all the complications with me, trying to help as best as she could. It wasn't easy, even for a nephrologist as the caregiver, to try to work within the healthcare system limitations.

Fumi is now my very best friend and I love her unconditionally. Given the tough medical cards I was dealt, she showed me ways to better align everyday choices with my life goals. One goal is to remain in this body for as long as possible. I now have good health and a great quality of life despite my four chronic diseases. I credit her role in my life as a big part of my well-being. I escaped deep depression because of my new friendship though I scored a 3 on the PHQ-9 depression screening questionnaire conducted at Mayo Clinic, denoting minimal depression. It would have been hard to go through being diagnosed and treated for kidney failure and cancer without support.

She too has grown because of our friendship. In addition to caring for kidney patients professionally, she now has the experience of living through the many challenges in the life of a dialysis and post-transplant patient firsthand, as my caregiver and friend. Her understanding of life with kidney disease is so much greater because of this roller coaster journey that she was willing to take with me. In addition, I've helped her see my perspective of life situations, as someone who has had to develop street smarts, as a Black man, a strong Christian, a small businessman, a veteran, a patient who will never give up, and an optimistic risk taker. Through me, she has broadened her own views in a number of areas where she had previously been naïve. While we agree to disagree on many topics, we have in our own ways grown immensely because our paths have crossed.

CHAPTER SEVEN

Transplant

I signed on with the local kidney transplant facility in Honolulu. Sereta, my youngest sister, volunteered to rescue me from dialysis by donating one of her kidneys. I love my sister and would do the same for her in a heartbeat. I feel there is no greater gift than an organ that anyone can give in this life. There is a rigorous kidney donor screening process that makes a lot of sense. They do not allow a person to donate their kidney unless laboratory results are normal. Also, if you have any sort of chronic disease or elevated blood pressure, you're out.

The St. Francis Medical Center dropped the ball when they did not respond to the doctor who was assessing whether my sister would be a good match as my kidney donor. At that time something told me to call Northwestern Memorial Hospital in Chicago. When I called and asked to be on their waiting list for kidney transplant donations, they immediately screened me over the phone. However, before I could be approved to join their kidney transplant program, I had to be evaluated at the hospital. I let out a deep sigh of relief when I found out that I had passed their prescreening. Within a couple of weeks my schedule of appointments for Northwestern arrived in the mail. I would need to stay in Chicago for three days to complete my appointments there. The hospital also contacted my nephrologist for my medical records and a limited amount of dialysis records in advance of my appointments. My review at Northwestern went as well as could be expected. I was placed on their kidney transplant list to receive a cadaver kidney because Northwestern discovered that my little sister did not qualify as a live donor for me. I was profoundly disappointed. Sereta was disqualified because her lab results showed the presence of a larger than normal amount of protein in her urine, which is always a red flag for potential health issues. Thankfully, Sereta says it's no longer an issue.

Two years after my hospital visit I was diagnosed with multiple myeloma. Although two hospitals had removed me from their kidney transplant wait lists, Northwestern Memorial wanted me to see their myeloma specialist before making a decision. Fumi and I together met with the specialist.

At Northwestern, Dr. Anthony Hauser, the myeloma specialist, told us that Northwestern believed in quality of life and under his guidance the hospital would transplant me even though I had multiple myeloma. There was one condition prior to receiving a transplant. I had to either complete a stem cell transplant or have my stem cells harvested and frozen for future use should I need them. I chose the second option. I returned to Northwestern six months later and had my stem cells harvested and frozen.

I hadn't expected the process to be so painful. In order to get my stem cells ready to be harvested, the hospital sent a supply of medication that was injected into my belly near the groin area three times a day for seven days. I could hardly walk when I deplaned in Chicago. After collecting my luggage, I took a cab to the hospital. Once we arrived at the hospital, I struggled to make my way inside the huge facility. I sat down on the first chair I could find and rested until I could muster up enough energy to check in.

The following morning a catheter — exactly like the dialysis bloodstream catheter I previously had had — was inserted into my neck. The stem cells were collected through a machine similar to the machine used for hemodialysis. The process took approximately four hours. Once the catheter was removed, I was immediately discharged from the hospital. I had a slight problem; I could barely walk. I called upon my cousin Rodney — a hospital policeman complete with a police badge, a firearm and a squad car — for help. He took me to my hotel room before we got something to eat and went to visit his mother, my aunt. I couldn't understand why I felt so groggy that I could barely stay awake during our conversation. After a couple of hours, my cousin took me to my hotel where I slept before catching an early flight home.

Fumi picked me at the airport and took me to her house, where I collapsed on the bedroom floor and stayed there for the next 24 hours. She looked at the area where the catheter had been and told me that blood was slowly dripping from the area and it didn't look good. The next day she took me to a local hospital where I was once again diagnosed with the mighty MRSA infection. The hospital released me because I was under Fumi's care. For several days she took care of me: preparing all my meals, giving me meds, taking my temperature and keeping me company. I was given the antibiotic vancomycin for the newly acquired MRSA during the last hour of my dialysis session for six weeks.

From that point on Northwestern Memorial stayed in contact with me quarterly. They monitored my health through monthly blood samples sent to their dialysis unit.

As the years passed, I slowly climbed up their transplant wait list. One day I got the call. The transplant coordinator called to discuss how I wanted to handle the coordination from Hawaii since I would need to be at Northwestern pronto after I receive the call for surgery. She told me that I could receive a transplant as soon as September, the following month. I told her I would call them in May of the following year to avoid spending winter in Chicago. The coordinator was fine with my decision. She suggested that I move to Chicago for a month during when they would prepare me to be ready to receive a kidney within 30 days. I was elated and incredibly thankful that I had finally made it to the top of Northwestern's waiting list! My gratitude went deep since I'd been booted off all the other kidney transplant lists once they had found out I had multiple myeloma. It was a dream coming true.

In May 2011, I called Northwestern Memorial's transplant coordinator to inform her of my arrival date in Chicago. We set an appointment to meet at the hospital shortly after my arrival. I was nearing the light at the end of my very long dialysis tunnel. This was definite proof my prayers and other people's prayers for me were being answered and that by believing and never giving up I will succeed no matter how high the odds are stacked against me.

While in Chicago, I stayed for two weeks in a hotel before moving into a downtown furnished condo. The condo was several long blocks from the hospital. I no longer minded the night shift dialysis schedule, which I continued three times a week in Chicago. I was looking forward to the end of dialysis treatment and to the beginning of returning to a more "normal" lifestyle. Two days after my arrival in Chicago my eldest sister, Lori, and her husband Bernard arrived to keep me company for a while. They checked into the same hotel where I was staying and we went shopping and sightseeing as if we were on vacation.

About three weeks after my arrival, I got a call from the transplant coordinator to discuss a kidney the hospital had earmarked for me. I was told the kidney was from a 21-year-old Hispanic man who had been murdered. She mentioned that it was a "high risk kidney." She explained that he'd been incarcerated at a youth correctional facility. I told her that a youth correctional facility wasn't the same as being jailed or imprisoned and that I would be very happy to accept the kidney. She thought it was a very good kidney and told me that I needed to be at the hospital within the hour to receive it.

I arrived at the hospital with only Lori, since her husband had to return to work. I was run through the normal hassle of signing into a hospital, given a hospital gown and shown to a private room. After I changed into the hospital gown, we waited about 20 minutes for the anesthesiologist to arrive. I was so grateful, happy and relieved that I was finally going to get a kidney transplant and get off dialysis! I was lying in the bed that had been wheeled just outside the operating room while we waited. When the anesthesiologist came, he shook my hand and said, "I know many people who are doing much worse than you." He then put a breathing mask over my mouth and told me to count backwards ... 10 ... 9 ... 8 ... . The last number I remembered was 7.

I was out for two-and-a-half hours. When I awoke there were four IVs attached to me. I looked over and saw Lori asleep on the couch. It was then that I realized I was back in my room. I looked at the area on my stomach where the surgery had taken place and saw metal staples. I was amazed that I just had major surgery and I felt very little pain. I thought, "Once the anesthesia wears off I'll feel it then for sure." Thankfully, the pain I was expecting never showed up. I'd felt more pain from some outpatient procedures than from the kidney transplant surgery.

Shortly after I awoke, my surgical team showed up to evaluate my progress. They asked me how I felt and wanted me to get up and walk around the ward. I did this by holding onto a rolling metal pole from where the IVs were suspended. The most unbelievable thing they said was, "We're sending you home tomorrow." Two of the most difficult things for me upon leaving the hospital the following day were simply standing and sitting. I was so stiff with pain that I needed Lori's help to put on my pants while I laid on the bed.

People who have kidney transplants will always get a catheter connected to their private parts. The catheter in my penis became infected within 48 hours after the operation. The body of the catheter was taped along my left leg. Every time I stepped with my left foot, I felt a bit of pain at the head of my penis where the catheter entered my body. I complained about it every time I went to the hospital — three times a week. The doctors said I had to live with it because there were no better alternatives. This lasted for about a week before the catheter was removed though the pain persisted even after it was gone. I continued to complain to Northwestern doctors about the pain in my penis and was eventually directed to complete some labs at the hospital which revealed that I had a urinary tract infection.

My New Normal

About two days after my transplant Lori returned to Mississippi and Fumi arrived to help me. Since the removal of the catheter, urinating became a new challenge. The last time I had actually urinated into a toilet was approximately six years prior. Since then my bladder had shrunk to about the size of a walnut from underuse. My new normal was being able to hold down liquids for about 10 to 15 minutes before I found myself running for a toilet. That meant a serious lack of sleep.

To my chagrin, I didn't always make it to the bathroom in time and would often wet myself. Lying in bed, I would feel the urge to go and within 20-30 seconds it became urgent. I couldn't sit straight up in bed because there were staples from the top of my groin area to just past my navel from the major surgery. Instead I had to roll over and let my feet hit the floor and I would notice urine slowly making it's way down my leg as my feet hit the floor. Even though I felt like I was still holding my urine. So I got the idea to ask for a plastic urinal and I could sleep in the reclined since the bed seemed to be high off the floor. Sleeping in the recliner worked much better, when the urge came, I simply stood up, relieved myself in the urinal, went into the bathroom and emptied it into the toilet and since this was happening every 15 minutes, I would drink a half bottle of water after each episode to replace the fluids I was emptying out of my body. I couldn't afford allowing my new transplanted kidney to become dehydrated. This vicious cycle went on for about two weeks before easing up and giving me a break.

I stayed in Chicago for six weeks following the transplant. By the time I returned home to Honolulu my bladder had expanded some. By then I was able to hold my urine twice as long for a grand total of 30 minutes before I faced the mad dash to a toilet. I found myself having to pull over often just to urinate. It was months later before things finally started to normalize.

Dr. Fumi Horita's explanation of my kidney transplanted catheter infection

Antonio developed a urinary tract infection from the foley catheter, a plastic tube that is inserted prior to transplant surgery into the bladder via his penis. Foley catheters are inserted using a sterile technique and are typically left in for several days after kidney transplantation and removed before the patient leaves the hospital. It is used to prevent urine from accumulating in the bladder, which would cause the bladder wall to stretch, risking a urine leak where the transplanted ureter was surgically connected to his bladder. Foley catheters can cause urine infections if inserted improperly, or if bacteria enter the urine while the catheter is in place.

Not only did Antonio have a bladder infection, his new kidney transplant was also involved. He had a ureteral stent — another plastic tube implanted during surgery — between the kidney and the bladder. This meant bacteria had infected his newly transplanted urinary tract.

In addition, newly transplanted patients are on the highest doses of immune system suppression medications to prevent rejection of their new organ. These medications also suppress your immune system from fighting infection.

Antonio was diagnosed with an Escherichia Coli (E.Coli) bacterial infection. Antibiotics were needed to kill the bacteria and the removal of all plastic, both catheter and stent, was required to resolve the infection. After several weeks of taking the appropriate antibiotic, his urine infection cleared. However, the antibiotic also killed healthy gut bacteria, allowing the bacteria Clostridium Difficile, also called C. diff to flourish. The bacteria produce a toxin that can cause colon inflammation and severe bloody diarrhea. Without appropriate antibiotic treatment, toxic megacolon can occur which could require a colon removal and a colostomy or could prove to be fatal.

The hospital slowly lowered my dosage of immunosuppressive medications as they sought to determine the most effective daily dosage for me. During this period I noticed a drastic increase in the number of bowel movements I experienced to the tune of once every 15 minutes which eventually turned into diarrhea. At first I blamed it on one of kidney transplant anti-rejection drugs, Myfortic (mycophenolic acid) which I took to keep my body from rejecting my new kidney.

This was a sudden change that happened on a Friday night around 6 p.m. in downtown Chicago. Because it was after hours I wasn't able to get a hold of a doctor immediately. I spoke with one of the nurses on duty at Northwestern and she wasn't able to get in contact with any doctors either. She advised us the best she could but the situation was outside her scope of expertise. I visited the toilet every 15 minutes through the following day. Around noon my longtime friend Terrell, who was caring for me after Fumi left, called the hospital again and again no doctors were available to consult. Three hours later we tried again but to no avail. A nurse from Northwestern recommended that I take Imodium for the diarrhea. When I asked her if she was certain that this approach was correct, she told me that it would at least provide some relief through the weekend. My gut warned me to not take the Imodium. I called Fumi to brief her on the situation and ask for her opinion. She asked if I had gotten a stool sample tested. I confirmed that indeed, I had already done so. She told me that I would need to complete three of them to rule out infection and that under no circumstance should I take Imodium.

I returned to the hospital on Monday and related what happened over the weekend to the lab personnel who told me that my lab results didn't show an infection. I told them that my nephrologist advised me to complete two more stool samples before the possibility of an infection could be ruled out. They agreed, so I completed a second stool sample and received a call from the hospital to let me know that I had an infection caused by the C. Diff bacteria. I was admitted into the hospital overnight where they started a course of treatment. I felt so much better the next morning and my bowel only moved once during my return flight to Honolulu that evening.

Maranatha Faith Center

CHAPTER EIGHT

Oozing from the Trenches

I was a young teenager, possibly 15 years old, when I first met Pastor Steve Jamison. My family had recently started attending the church where Jamison pastored. It was a small facility that could seat possibly 100 to 200 people. The building had been used as a preschool prior to Jamison securing a loan to purchase it. My mother told me that they and about four other families were co-signers on the loan. They all met Pastor Jamison one afternoon at a downtown bank where each of them signed the documents and given a copy for their records. They were really good folks trying to help found the church. This transaction was totally unknown to me at the time. Shortly after the loan was secured, I was offered a part-time job at one of Jamison's construction sites and performed manual labor at a fire station Jamison was building in Tupelo, Mississippi. This was my first job and lasted about two weeks until I returned to school. My family continued attending this Maranatha Faith Center for a few more years until Pastor Jamison bought a larger church facility on the opposite side of north Columbus.

Jamison had wanted to purchase a larger church with more land even though he hadn't been able to fill the seats in the smaller church. The larger church wasn't far away and was a good deal considering the size of the building. Unbeknownst to him, the reason for the discounted price was because the owners knew the grounds were totally contaminated with creosote. Jamison later found this out.

The bank permitted Jamison to occupy the larger church before the loan was completed and approved. About two weeks after moving in he called a meeting to announce to the congregation that he was raising tithes from 10 percent to 20 percent per member or family. Jamison gave no reason why he was raising the tithes to 20 percent and, according to my mother, Jamison told the church members, "I am asking you to do this as your leader and you are supposed to follow your leader." Jamison told the congregation that he needed their signatures as a guarantee that they would pay the 20 percent tithe. The Maranatha Faith members were then presented with a blank sheet of paper where they were to sign. There was no contract or any wording written on the sheet of paper. This dubious act alone would have raised a red flag for me. My mother believes that it was likely because the bank wanted to know who was going to be responsible for the mortgage with so few church members.

Prudently, my parents refused. Some people decided to leave the church rather than sign a blank piece of paper. Even though they did not sign, my parents continued to attend the new Maranatha Faith Center. Pastor Jamison started to increase the pressure on church members who refused to sign the blank sheet of paper by mailing repeated requests for a signature to guarantee a 20 percent tithe. Most of the members could barely pay the 10 percent as suggested in the bible (New King James Malachi 3: 8-10). My parents remained firm in their refusal. Jamison's next tactic to pressure my parents into signing was to exclude my parents from singing solo during church services and to bar my stepfather from preaching. This saddened both my parents. At this point they decided that their time was up at Maranatha Faith Center and they too left the church.

The following year my stepfather received a 1099 from the Internal Revenue Service (IRS) to pay taxes on earned income from Jamison's construction company. Totally shocked my stepfather called the IRS and explained to the IRS agent that as an employee he worked under a foreman at Jamison's construction company. The IRS agent explained to him that even though he's not a contractor, he would still need to pay the Social Security tax due for the income earned. The agent told him not to worry about paying the taxes on the letter he received. They were going to make Jamison pay them. Everybody was poor and had little money. On the other hand, Steve Jamison was a young entrepreneur and a church pastor, and he was trying to lead people who were, in many instances, much older, significantly wiser and more experienced than he was about handling the church's business. With cash flow being tight, he made some unfortunate mistakes that caused a few church members to move on in search of alternative spiritual leadership.

Denials Begin

On a cold wintry day in 1999, Jamison was digging ditches and preparing for the expansion of his church. The process of digging unearthed a gooey black substance that turned out to be creosote, a wood preservative.[5] Being unfamiliar with the substance, Jamison continued to work in

---

5 Janice Francis-Smith, "Legal, fiscal woes leave Tronox future uncertain", *The Journal Record*, November 4, 2008

the presence of the black goo until it was too late. "When I came out the ditch, I had blood pressure that was so high, I had to take two pills four times a day to control it. I learned that my kidneys dropped in function to almost a third of their normal function. At that point, I realized whatever it was, was deadly and dangerous."[6] Presently, Steve Jamison is a dialysis patient.

The following year Jamison brought a lawsuit[7] against the Kerr McGee Chemical Company for the creosote contamination of his property. He charged that the hazardous substance released by the company had interfered with his and his family's use and enjoyment of the property and that Jamison and his lawyers wanted legal and equitable remedies. Jamison also named the Mississippi Department of Environmental Quality (MDEQ) as a defendant. However, with MDEQ, Jamison and his attorneys only wanted equitable resolutions and not monetary awards. I was told that Kerr McGee offered Jamison $3 million to settle. That settlement stipulated that he had to remain silent about the creosote contamination affair and the settlement offer. After Jamison refused the initial offer, Kerr McGee upped the ante to $4.5 million with the same stipulation. Jamison turned down that offer because he felt — as a pastor — it was wrong to suppress the truth.

Jamison eventually won about 8 million in mid-2018 for the Maranatha Faith Center, after nearly 20 years of negotiating in the courts.

Jamison knew his land was still contaminated after Kerr-McGee finished its clean up. He thought that the MDEQ — where he submitted his creosote contamination report — would help him get his property cleaned up. And they did help, but not completely. In July 1999, in response to Jamison's request, MDEQ investigated "off-site drainage ditches downgrade of the facility [Kerr-McGee plant]."[8] The samples, extracted from a depth of 12 inches, indicated the presence of pentachlorophenol (PCP)

---

6   Victoria Bailey, "VIDEO: Residents Finally Receiving Settlement Money From Kerr-McGee Suit", *WCBI News*, June 6, 2017, https://www.wcbi.com/video-residents-finally-receiving-settlement-money-kerr-mcgee-suit/

7   Maranatha Faith Center, Inc., Plaintiff, vs. Kerr-McGee Corp., Kerr-McGee Chemical, LLC, Moss-American, Inc., T.J. Moss Tie Company, American Creosoting, Inc., Mississippi Department of Environmental Quality, Sanderson Plumbing Products, Inc., Columbus Cemetery and Investment Co., and Fictitious Parties A, B and C, Civil Action No. 62000-294, Ch. of the FJD of Hinds County, MS, 2000

8   U.S. Dept. of Health and Human Services, Public Health Service. 2014. *ATSDR Public Health Assessment for Kerr-McGee Chemical Corporation (a/k/a Tronox, Inc.) Columbus, Lowndes County, Mississippi EPA Facility I.D. MSD990866329 JUNE 12, 2014.* The ATSDR Public Health Assessment, 15. https://www.atsdr.cdc.gov/hac/pha/Kerr-McGeeChemical-Corporation/Kerr-McGee_Tronox,%20Inc_PHA_Final_06-12-2014.pdf

and Benzo(a)pyrene (BaP).[9] Later in the same year MDEQ issued an order requiring Kerr-McGee Chemical Corporation to clean up Jamison's land. The huge chemical corporation ignored MDEQ's order and completely shirked their responsibility to clean up the toxic mess. The city of Columbus paved the ditch where Jamison found creosote and claimed the ditch as government property. Jamison had watched the government employees pave over the ditch and didn't see them clean up the contamination prior to paving.

Kerr-McGee's lawyers screamed case closed since the trench had been paved over and no other contamination was evident.

Taking on the Big Dogs

As Jamison searched for ways to prove the continued contamination of his property, a friend mentioned Tennie White. White is a black American woman who has spent most of her career exposing environmental contamination. She has been closely embroiled with significant cases that involved large-scale industrial pollution and led to millions of dollars in cleanup expenses.

Tennie White initially cut her teeth in the environmental industry during her employment at Environmental Protection Systems, where she was hired in the early 1980s. After ten years with the company and some time at a metal finishing company, White decided to head out on her own. She started an environmental laboratory that focused on removing asbestos and conducting tests for contamination at industrial sites.

White helped Jamison expose the creosote and other contaminants to the EPA. Even though the city of Columbus had warned Jamison that the paved-over trench was now city property, he still hopped into a backhoe and dug into the trench to confirm the continued presence of creosote on his land.

The EPA conducted three rounds of soil sampling between 2010 and early 2011. They included two samples from an unsecured soil pile generated

---

9   PCP was first manufactured in the 1930s and among other things was used as a pesticide, disinfectant and wood preservative. It is a chemical that does not occur naturally and became unavailable to the general public in 1984. BaP occurs as it is formed during incomplete combustion of organic material — think forest fires and charred meats — but it is also man-made. It can be found in places such as asphalt and coal-tar production plants.

by the removal of the concrete in the culvert that Jamison had dug up. In March 2011 the EPA gave a final research-based report that stated six carcinogenic, semi-volatile organic compound levels exceeded their suggested action levels often by more than six times. One of the contamination locations was the athletic field at Hunt Intermediate School where I attended the 7th grade. The EPA noted contamination at a 90-acre tract combined with a superfund site[10] the fall of 2011. Some $67 million was expected in clean-up costs which includes the removal of more than 50,000 tons of contaminated soil by the project's completion which is expected to continue for a number of years.

Though testing for creosote contamination in Columbus, Mississippi began in the 2000s it can be certain that environmental pollution in the area had been present decades prior. The Mississippi Department of Natural Resources notified Kerr-McGee, as early as 1989, of "a serious water problem with the large number of ditches that drain contaminants off the plant property. Rainwater washes creosote off the stored crossties and drains uncontrolled into the ditches surrounding the plant that run through the adjoining neighborhoods including properties of residents, churches and businesses where people live and children play."[11] It can be certain that in addition, water from the heavy rains that frequent Columbus — rains that also create flooding — contribute to the spread of the contaminants from the Kerr-McGee plant.

There are residential properties no further than 100 feet from the Kerr-McGee facility. Furthermore there are unlined, open drainage ditches throughout neighborhoods adjacent to the facility. The land around the Kerr-McKee facility as well as the main waterway in the area, Luxapalila Creek — where I used to fish — remain well-used. Within a one-mile radius there are businesses, minority and low-income housing, six public schools and many daycare facilities. The creek is situated a half mile from the facility and is the largest perennial drainage in the area. In addition, according to a 2014 public health assessment report by the Agency

---

10   Congress created the designation of "Superfund site" in 1980 to allow the EPA to clean up sites contaminated by improperly managed hazardous substances. Superfund is the informal designation for The Comprehensive Environmental Response, Compensation and Liability Act (CERCLA). CERCLA also enables the EPA to force parties responsible for contamination to either reimburse the government for cleanup work or to perform cleanups on their own. https://EPA.gov/superfund/what-superfund

11   Maranatha Faith Center, Inc., Plaintiff, vs. Kerr-McGee Corp., Kerr-McGee Chemical, LLC, Moss-American, Inc., T.J. Moss Tie Company, American Creosoting, Inc., Mississippi Department of Environmental Quality, Sanderson Plumbing Products, Inc., Columbus Cemetery and Investment Co., and Fictitious Parties A, B and C, Civil Action No. 62000-294, Ch. of the FJD of Hinds County, MS, 2000

Figure 1. Demographic Profile of 1 mile and 3 mile radius of the Kerr-McGee Site

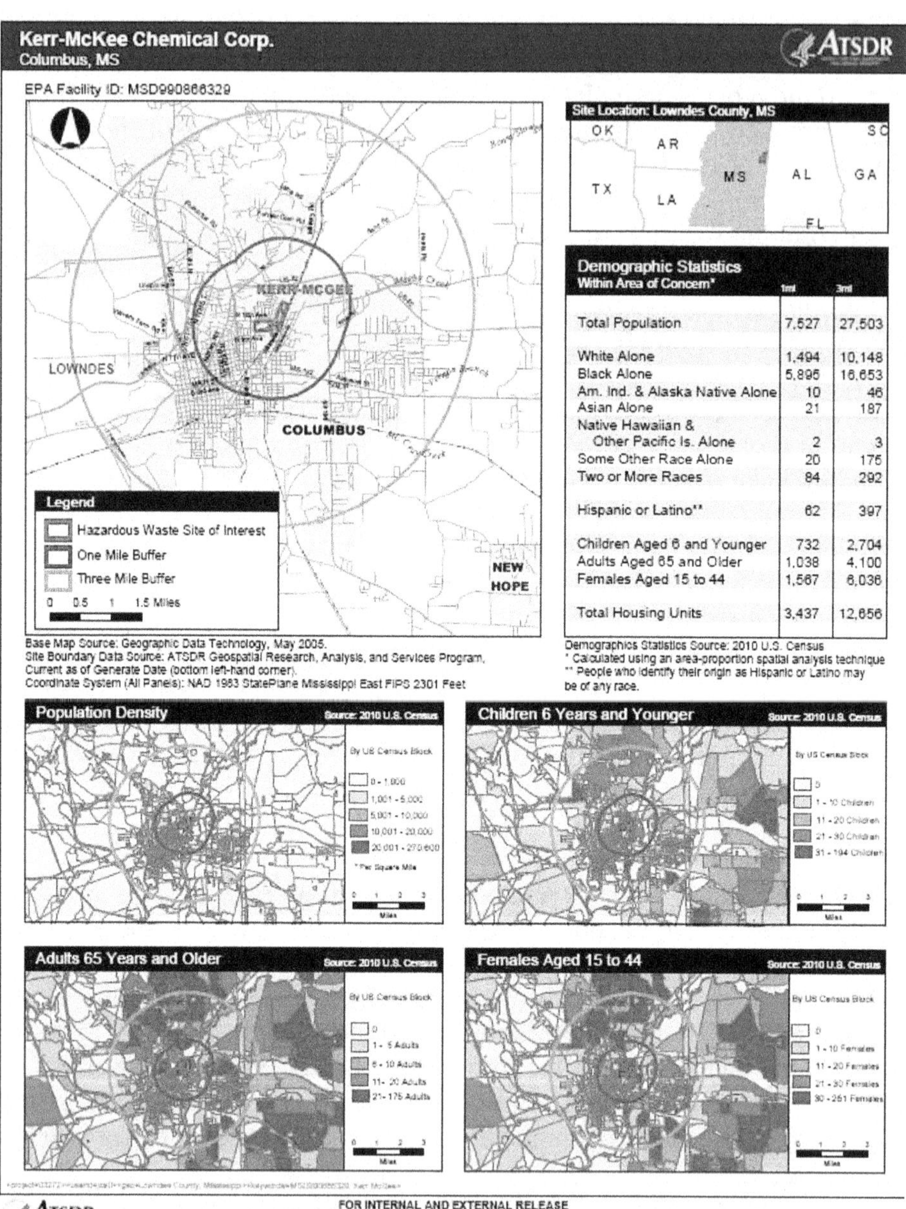

Demographic Statistics Within Area of Concern*	1mi	3mi
Total Population	7,527	27,503
White Alone	1,494	10,148
Black Alone	5,895	16,653
Am. Ind. & Alaska Native Alone	10	46
Asian Alone	21	187
Native Hawaiian & Other Pacific Is. Alone	2	3
Some Other Race Alone	20	175
Two or More Races	84	292
Hispanic or Latino**	62	397
Children Aged 6 and Younger	732	2,704
Adults Aged 65 and Older	1,038	4,100
Females Aged 15 to 44	1,567	6,036
Total Housing Units	3,437	12,656

Figure 1. Demographic Profile of 1 mile and 3 mile radius of the Kerr-McGee Site, UU.S. Dept. of Health and Human Services, Public Health Service. 2014. *ATSDR Public Health Assessment for Kerr-McGee Chemical Corporation (a/k/a Tronox, Inc.) Columbus, Lowndes County, Mississippi EPA Facility I.D. MSD990866329 JUNE 12, 2014.* The ATSDR Public Health Assessment, 11. https://www.atsdr.cdc.gov/hac/pha/Kerr-McGeeChemicalCorporation/Kerr-McGee_Tronox,%20Inc_PHA_Final_06-12-2014.pdf

for Toxic Substances and Disease Registry, the portion of the Luxapalila Creek sitting upstream of the Kerr-McGee facility is categorized as a public water supply. The portion of the creek downstream is designated for fishing and wildlife and includes activities such as swimming and wading. Use of the creek has most likely increased after a state fly-fishing record for spotted bass was set at Luxapalila Creek in 2004.

The biggest disappointment to many (not all) of the white citizens of Columbus was that while Kerr-McGee lied, defended and concealed every creosote spill on the north side of Columbus until the very end, they never imagined that the contamination would spill over and reach East Columbus where the most prominent business owners, doctors and lawyers and bankers lived. The discovery of creosote in East Columbus' Propst Park was seemingly kept under wraps for the most part. However, it's possible that many of the white homeowners in East Columbus were aware of this as they chose to sell their homes below market value shortly after.

Many of the black citizens were unaware the contamination had reached the well-manicured lawns and the underground water supply of East Columbus. I was blown away when my mother told me my step-father's sister had bought a home in East Columbus. I told her I couldn't wait to see her home during my next visit. It was one of the very first places my parents took me to visit and at no time were the words "contamination" and "creosote" mentioned. In fact, none of my immediate family or friends knew or even suspected that the contamination had spread to East Columbus. Many black residents thought they were "moving on up" as they started occupying the neighborhoods that were once out of their reach.

CHAPTER NINE

Kerr-McGee

The company once known as Kerr-McGee was an American company founded in 1929 by Oklahoma entrepreneur James L. Anderson and his brother-in-law Robert S. Kerr. They called it the Anderson & Kerr Drilling Company. The oil industry was booming, the Great Depression had not hit yet, and Kerr, who was an attorney at the time, abandoned his law practice to take advantage of the oil rush. Kerr's affluence and influence grew until he later became the governor of Oklahoma and a U.S. Senator. When James Anderson retired in 1936 Kerr lured Dean A. McGee, former chief geologist for Phillips Petroleum, to join the firm as vice president for production and exploration the following year. In 1946, McGee was promoted to executive vice-president and the company was rebranded Kerr-McGee Oil Industries, Inc. McGee remained a key figure in the company and went on to become its president, chief executive officer and chairman of the board.

Over time the company focused its international operations mainly on oil and natural gas production, inorganic industrial chemicals and coal mining. At its peak, Kerr-McGee had its hands in nearly every energy enterprise conceivable — gasoline, coal, uranium, plutonium, chemicals, oil drilling, forestry, natural gas and perchlorate. It was essentially a one-stop energy shop. The company had international interests in oil exploration and production in Australia, Indonesia, the Gulf of Mexico, the South China Sea and China's Bohai Bay. Additionally, it had plants in Saudi Arabia, the Netherlands and other European countries.

Kerr-McGee purchased its first refinery in 1945 and in 1955 it purchased the refining and pipeline marketing operations of the Deep Rock Oil Corporation along with more than 800 retail oil and gas stations in 16 states.

To say that Kerr-McGee was a menace to humanity would be putting it lightly. Their business practices created ticking time bombs and the EPA as well as OSHA should have thoroughly investigated their many operations and considered them for shut down. It seems that many of their sites were either a disasters in the making or the sites had already become environmental catastrophes which Kerr-McGee management were actively covering up. In 1952, Kerr-McGee started mining for uranium in the Lukachukai Mountains in Navajo Nation[12] and elsewhere. Though by that time the dangers of uranium were known, none of the miners were equipped with any safety equipment. They were surrounded by radioactive material within the mines, breathing in radioactive dust and their communities were bathed in radioactive waste in its many forms. The company bought American Potash & Chemical Company in 1967[13] which owned a facility in Las Vegas that produced ammonium perchlorate, commonly used as a component of rocket fuel, among other things. From this facility perchlorate was found to have contaminated surface water from Las Vegas Wash to Lake Mead and down onto the lower Colorado River. Not only was surface water affected but the ground water beneath the facility was as well. The company also owned a facility that produced radioactive thorium since the 1930s on the west side of Chicago, Illinois. The radioactive byproduct was dumped in an exposed mound and added to over decades, eventually garnering the name Mount Thorium. The enormous mound, which at one point measured roughly 500,000 cubic yards, was finally removed after the city threatened to pass legislation to remove it.[14]

The company bought TJ Moss Tie Company in 1963 and at this time owned and operated 15 wood-treating creosote plants and had created 18 additional creosote plants across the country. In 1998 Kerr-McGee expanded into titanium dioxide (TiO2)[15] and acquired plants in Savannah, Georgia; Bostik, Netherlands; Antwerp, Belgium; and Uerdingen, Germany. With these acquisitions Kerr-McGee became the third largest producer in the world of TiO2.

Kerr-McGee was now a giant in the oil exploration and chemical businesses — easily pulling in well over $1 billion in revenue per year — but was a small fry when it came to clean up and was equally negligent when enforcing safety measures to keep its plant operations and employees safe.

---

12   Wilbert Leland Dare. 1961. *Uranium Mining in the Lukachai Mountains, Apache County, Ariz., Kerr-McGee Oil Industries, inc.* Washington: U.S. Dept. of the Interior, Bureau of Mines.
13   Clare M. Reckert, "American Potash in agreement for merger with Kerr-McGee; AMERICAN POTASH AGREES TO MERGE Rapid-American Leeds Travelwear," *New York Times*, (New York, NY), July 15, 1967. https://www.nytimes.com/1967/07/15/archives/american-potash-in-agreement-for-merger-with-kerrmcgee-american.html
14   Andis Robeznieks, "West Chicago vs. Kerr-McGee — Warning: Exposure to Hazardous Wastes Can Cause Community Activism," *Chicago Reader* (Chicago, IL), June 6, 1991. https://www.chicagoreader.com/chicago/assault-on-mount-thorium/Content?oid=877745
15   Titanium dioxide is an industrial chemical with a multitude of uses that is often added to foods, personal care products, and many other commonly used products. E.g. To whitening paints, paper, plastic and other products; anti-caking agent in powders; to create abrasiveness; in sunscreen to block the sun's radiation.

Navajo Nation

A case study of the Navajo Indian relationship with Kerr-McGee highlights a prevailing attitude of negligence. In the early 1950s, Kerr-McGee hired Navajo Indians to mine for uranium on Navajo land at a time when the United States was stockpiling nuclear weapons. This was long before the establishment of the Occupational Safety and Health Administration (OSHA) in 1970. OSHA is a United States governmental agency under the Department Of Labor, whose job is to enforce standards and training for the establishment and maintenance of a healthful and safe work environment.

Kerr-McGee repeatedly lied and withheld the truth about the dangers of uranium to the Navajos. The company frequently reinforced the lie that mining uranium was harmless while sending their workers unprotected into the mines. Without OSHA in place, no health, safety or pollutant guidelines were available to be followed. According to interviews conducted by Tom Barry, an energy writer for the Navajo Time reveal some of the working conditions the Navajo were subjected to. One miner said, "They chased us in there like we were slaves." John H. Lee recalled how "It made us sick to go into those mines at Cove. The white men sat outside the mines and pushed us Navajos into those dusty mines right after dynamiting." "I remember that it used to be so dusty that we were always spitting up black stuff and how we went home we all had headaches from breathing all that contamination!" recalled another miner.[16] Kerr-McGee was one of the first companies to use the Navajo to mine uranium. It was responsible for the welfare and safety of all its workers anytime they were engaged in official company business.

Kerr-McGee and many other private companies descended upon the Navajo nation and states outside Navajo land as well. According to an August 2014 Department Of Energy report to Congress, a total of 4,225 mines provided uranium ore to the AEC, Atomic Energy Commission from 1947 to 1970. 26 of these mines could not be located for proper closure. Approximately 69 percent of the mines were in Colorado and Utah and the balance were in Arizona, New Mexico and Wyoming. A total of 75.9 million total tons of uranium ore was produced for defense related purposes. New Mexico led with more than 35 million tons, followed by Colorado, Utah and Wyoming each with 11 million tons. Nearly half of the mines

---

16   Tom Barry, "The Navajo lung cancer widows," Navajo Times (Window Rock, AZ), August 24, 1978.

were located on federal land managed by the U.S. Bureau of Land Management. Approximately 11 percent of the mines were on Tribal Lands.

The Navajos were then living, breathing and drinking radiation as radioactive waste, or tailings, were stored above ground and contaminated water overflowed from the mines. The water that seeped out of unusual places looked crystal clear and drinkable.[17] The Navajos used the water for cooking, cleaning and drinking while their children played in the pools of crystal clear water that formed outside the mines and played inside the closed, but unsealed and still radioactive mines.

Radioactive tailings still scattered over Navajo land to this day produce Radon gas that easily travels with the lightest winds, thereby contaminating lands — including plants, animals and people who live off the land — thousands of miles away. Health risk from uranium exposure cuts like a knife from the men and boys who worked in the mines, to the women who were mothers and wives who washed the clothes of miners that was also contaminated.

Failing health is still one of the biggest concerns that remains a constant nightmare for more than 173,000 Navajo Indians. "We are not isolated in our struggle with uranium development" John Redhouse said, who was the associate director of the Albuquerque — based National Indian Youth Council. "Many Indian people are now supporting the struggles of the Australian Aborigines and the Black Indigenous people of Namibia (South West Africa) against similar uranium developments. We have recognized that we are facing the same international beast."[18]

Residents' Testimonies

Kerr-McGee's apathy toward its responsibilities to the environment and people extended to residents who lived nearby. The following testimonies from some of these residents describe Kerr-McGee's willful neglect and uncaring attitude for the safety and well-being of the residents of Columbus, Mississippi. The Kerr-McGee chemical plant in my hometown was

---

17   Laurel Morales, "For the Navajo Nation, Uranium mining's deadly legacy lingers", *Weekend Edition Sunday,* NPR, April 10, 2016, https://www.npr.org/sections/health-shots/2016/04/10/473547227/for-the-navajo-nation-uranium-minings-deadly-legacy-lingers
18   Bruce E. Johansen, "The High Cost Of Uranium In Navajoland," *Akwesasne Notes New Series,* Volume 2 #2, April May June, 1997, pp10-12, https://ratical.org/radiation/UraniumInNavLand.html.

so corrosive to the environment and the surrounding community that someone should have reported to the EPA that the plant was a time bomb that needed to be closed and cleaned up immediately. If only someone had pieced together the puzzle of our childhood ailments along with the plants pollution decades ago so much pain and suffering could have been avoided. ...

Terrell and I are still close friends. We talk on the phone a few times a month and text and e-mail each other frequently. I offered Terrell the first opportunity to talk about his life, his health and how being exposed to the harmful substance creosote has affected his life. Here Terrell gives testimony about living in Morningside Apartments.

Jerry Terrell Petty *I spoke with Terrell by telephone in March, 2019.*

We inhaled toxic fumes blown in from the creosote plant about four blocks away. I was never able to distinguish my playground from the contaminated site. The border of the site had no barricade or enclosure; nothing related to the deadly site was covered or underground to indi-cate the danger was of such an enormous magnitude — some days the odor was extremely strong and unbearable, making breathing very hard and toxic to the body; our eyes would burn, often appearing teary and red. We had no idea at the time that the plant could be the source of our childhood ailments: the rashes, the headaches, the labored breathing and numerous other complications.

Terrell went on to tell his story about his current medical condition.

I'm living in the reality of the harmful effects of living on top of contam-inants. The devastation and deterioration to my health has become more evident with each passing year. Over the years, I've suffered allergies, rashes, nosebleeds, unexplained swelling and excessive tiredness but the most severe problems I am currently experiencing are the results of congestive heart failure — and its complications — at the age of 42, what should have been my most vital and productive years. I recently had a brain stroke which has compromised and complicated matters more, worsening my health to the point that I am no longer able to do simple tasks, with impaired motor skills, nerve damage, periodic swelling (body retaining water) shortness of breath, and an impaired memory. I cannot recall a time where I have felt this helpless, now requiring assistance.

Making matters more distressful, the compensation and hope for res-
titution promised has not come — except for three small incremental
subsidy payments. It's a hardship, both physically and financially to me
and my family. No one that has been tragically affected by this situation
should have to experience this level of personal pain and grief.

Eric Collins *I spoke with Eric by telephone in March, 2019.*

Eric tells me he's originally from Bridgeport, Connecticut and his parents
moved to Columbus when he was only four-years-old. They moved to the
North side and resided on 24th Street which was just four blocks from
the Kerr-McGee chemical plant. A few years later, his parents moved from
24th Street to 27th Street North, a move that put them even closer to the
chemical plant. According to Eric they lived very close to the area that
Kerr-McGee employees called the pine yard which was one of the two
shipping yards the company operated. He recalls frequently playing on
contaminated stored inventory the company had left unsecured during
his childhood. Eric's health problems cut deep and permanent. Losing his
daughter at age 35 to breast cancer was heartbreaking. He recalls, "I used
to walk my daughter to and from school — often cutting through the pine
yard." Eric has suffered from high blood pressure, high cholesterol, and
prostate cancer and sinus illnesses for the past five years.

Eric is one of tens of thousands of future tort claimants from around
the country who are waiting to receive a monetary settlement from the
Kerr-McGee/Tronox trustee, Garretson Resolution Group, based in Ohio.[19]
Since settlement checks have stalled for the past year, Eric wanted to
unify the city's injured people to protest the complete interruption of
settlement checks flowing to Columbus's residents. He organized and
led a march on October 14, 2018 at 6 p.m. CST. The march started at
Wells Cleaners, near 21st Street and continued to 27th Street near Eric's
childhood home. The march was intentionally cut short so the elderly
and those in poor health wouldn't have too far to walk, especially since it
was a cold fall day. The march strategically passed by the site where the
Kerr-McGee plant once stood.

---

19   Garretson Resolution Group is a law firm that specializes in offering administrative services of complex settlements to thousands of law firms (defense and plaintiffs),
corporations and government agencies.

Sherita Deloach *I spoke with Sherita by telephone in June, 2019.*

Sherita, now 27 years of age, grew up with her mother on the north side of Columbus right next to the Kerr-McGee plant on 22nd Street. There she played outside on land that has now been designated as contaminated. Sherita said that black patches the size of a quarter started to appear on her body when she was just 17-years-old. The first black patch was on her neck; then the patches spread to the fold in her arm and from there to her legs and feet. As time passed, the condition worsened. When she was 21 the patches enlarged and became more difficult to treat on her own. Her entire hand and fingertips blistered where spotty blood also appeared that became quite painful for days and nights, limiting sleep and work.

Today, Sherita also has a black patch across the top of her forehead. Her condition has been diagnosed as eczema. Her co-pay is $60-$100 with insurance for treatment creams and steroids to treat it. Her doctors told her that eczema is incurable and that she will have it for the rest of her life. Sherita told me during our telephone discussion that the Garretson Resolution Group rejected her claim. I advised her to refile the claim, this time with the trustee and to also send a copy to Judge Michael E. Wiles at the U.S. Bankruptcy Court Southern District of New York.

Kerr McGee Employee Testimonies[20]

Mark Finch 10-Year Kerr-McGee Employee, Shipping Supervisor

We had one (a spill) when all of corporate was there. They hit a pipe and creosote was just flooding out the back gate while we were in the middle of a meeting. They went running out there and they put down what they call Y Socks trying to absorb some of it up but it was flowing out of a 2-inch pipe out the back gate as fast as it could go. So they ended digging up the ground out there behind the back gate and all kind of stuff, you know? Trying to stop it before it got into the water supply and ended up getting the pipe stopped and everything you know.

Question: So now you said corporate was down, you mean the corporate Kerr-McGee corporate people?

---

20   Kerr-McGee employee testimonies were found on YouTube.com. Search for "Columbus Creosote" 1A, 1B, 1C. wmv, 2A and 2C.

Finch: Right. Bob Mikkel, Jim Sanders ... they were all there for a meeting. They usually came down once or twice a year and had a meeting with the whole plant, telling us where ... as a matter of fact we were having a safety and environmental meeting then. They come down and tell you all about safety, all about environmental, how the company doing as a whole and they were all there then ... Greg Alexander, Jim Sanders, Bob Mikkel. They were all there then.

Question: So somebody hits a pipe and what do the corporate guys do?

Finch: Panicked! Ha-ha pretty much. When they come in and told them there's creosote running out the back gate everybody just stopped the meeting, everybody went outside and started trying to get it up as fast as we could you know.

Question: Now we heard that story from someone else and they said they had gone home that night and they saw the plant manager on television saying, "We had a small spill today, maybe a gallon got away." Do you recall any of that?

Finch: Yes, I remember. Yes. But there was a river flowing out the back gate. (Chuckle)

Question: So the plant manager basically went on television and lied?

Finch: Evidently, yes. (laughs)

Question: When you say a river, you estimate for me how much creosote got away.

Finch: Well, a 55-gallon drum, I mean that just to give you an idea of how much creosote. So you know a lot of people know what a 55-gallon drum is okay? They filled up at least 10 of those trying to get it gathered up. So there was at least 10 of those within a few minutes period. And that's not counting the dirt that was contaminated the stuff going up into the water supply.

Question: So, you're saying over 500 gallons?

Finch: Correct.

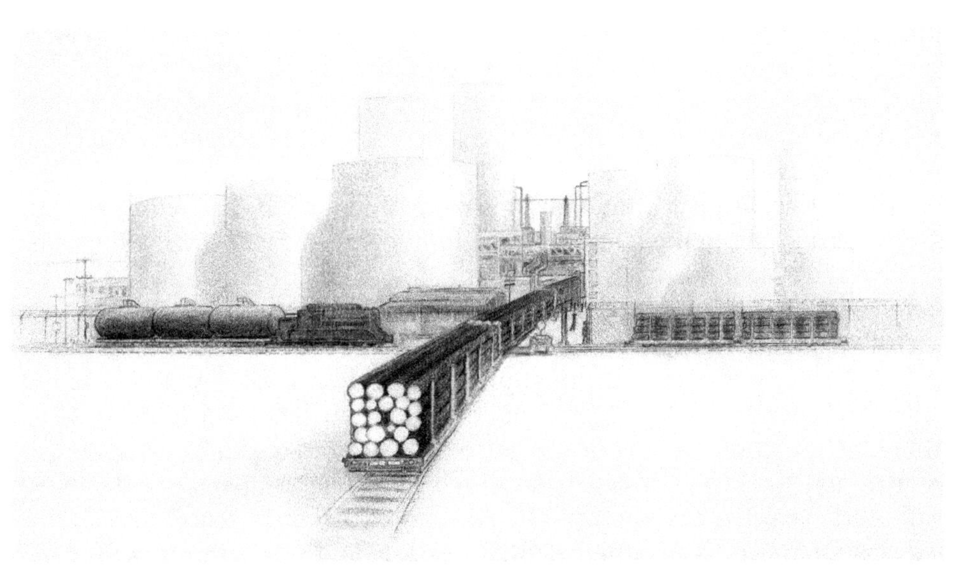

Kerr McGee facilities in Columbus, MS

Question: That was a major spill!

Finch: Major spill, yes.
     I filled out a treated storage yard report, like I said before; it states if you have over one pound of drippage in the yard, you're supposed to notify (call) the plant manager who is supposed to notify the EPA there's been a violation. I talked to the manager several times about how we fill out the report and it's not right. He said things need to be done the way they are being done and it's not a good career move to talk about it.
     I have pictures that can show you that when it rained it looked like a creosote lake out there. From there it drained into the ditches, from the ditches it has to go to the streams and rivers because that's where it naturally flows.
     So yes, I mean ... many times what should've happened — you know you're asking me my job as a shipping supervisor — one thing, we receive the creosote treated material off the drippage pan okay, when it comes out of the cylinders. Those treated crossties are supposed to sit on those pads until they do not drip anymore. That's the rules, alright? A lot of times because of production reasons they say, "Hey, we gotta get this stuff changed out and get it off the pads so we can get more stuff in there." They would go ahead and push it down into each shipping department — one on the pine yard side which was across the street 14th Avenue, and the other one on my side. So we had two different yards. There was called a Norfolk Southern yard and a Burlington Northern yard, two different railroads. So some of that stuff would go across the street and some would come on my side.
     A lot of times that stuff was still dripping creosote on the ground because it hadn't been evaporated off or, you know, been cleaned off. When they push it down into that department, you know, it just drips all over the ground, you know? And those trams, they were called trams, that hold those crossties. You know a tram would hold probably a couple of gallons of creosote in them. There were numerous reports that we gave, you know, to management about these trams leaking, you know, gallons of creosote every day onto the ground you know. They said well, we know about it and we're trying to do something about it.

Question: Now you say management, who specifically would you say know about it?

Finch: Ron Murphy and Chuck Swan. Chuck Swan was over the environmental part. He was the treating supervisor and the assistant plant manager at the end, and Ron was plant manager at the end.

Question: You think corporate knew about this in Oklahoma?

Finch: Oh yes! At the end, I know they did because I also sent them pictures to ask them about that. I sent them the pictures toward the end of the plant and asked them, you know, you know this is going on down here. What do you think about this? And it was very quiet from their end.

The cylinders were about 100 feet long and about 25-30 feet in diameter. And that if you could imagine how much creosote it would hold, many thousand gallons of creosote, and sometimes the doors were concave in shape, and they had gaskets in these doors. Under the pressure sometimes those gaskets would blow and it was because those doors were not properly aligned a lot of times is why those gaskets would blow.

And the maintenance department ... and the management department knew about the doors not being aligned properly. And they would just keep replacing gaskets in those doors, and they keep blowing, and when they did blow, it would blow creosote into the air and blow it all over the ground. It was a lot of creosote. It would cover the employees' parking lot which was probably about 200 to 300 feet away from the cylinders. And they would have to pay to get the cars washed and painted.

You think about this okay? You think about 100 feet of crossties come out of one cylinder, okay? Three times a day. You got three cylinders alright? So you talking about three hundred feet of crossties three times a day comes out of a cylinder.

A lot of times, they don't sit on the pad so they going down to the departments. At least these hundred foot long charges may sit on this railroad track all night long so when we get there in the morning, creosote done run all off of them, all over the ground, all everywhere, okay? Alright? So when we get there in the morning we have to unload those charges and put them up. So then all this creosote is on the ground. So they bought this little tractor and this little rake. You just ride through there and rake it into the ground. We did that all the time, you know and you figure for a period of how many years that went on. Puddles of creosote on top of puddles of creosote on the ground.

Question: It just soaks on down into the ground?

Finch: Right, soaks unless it rains. If it rains, it washes it right off into the ditch right then. That happens a lot of times. It's like a river sometimes because of the way the yard was laid out. All the water from the framing mill which was all the way at the far end gate where the treatment plant was, alright, it comes. All the water from the treating department would come all down to the plant, into shipping, into that ditch behind shipping that ditch and then it ran into 14th Avenue, right there. That's the ditch that ran into 14th Avenue.

Question: So 14th Avenue it was literally a creosote river sometimes?

Finch: That's right.

Jerry Lewis Brooks 15-Year Kerr-McGee Employee

I saw my plant manager go on TV and lie.

Question: Who is your plant manager?

Brooks: [Gives the name.]

Question: What did he lie about?

Brooks: One day we were having a meeting and all the big people were having a meeting [from] Oklahoma had come here and we went to dinner that night. One guy was working with a backhoe. He backed into a pipe and busted it at the front gate next to the club Flamingo. Creosote went all down a water drain. When I got home, my wife told me your company was on the news tonight. I stepped out of the shower to look at the TV. He stood up there and said we spilled about 5 gallons, man we probably cleaned up about 250 gallons of creosote, we started at about 12 am and finished about 5 pm.

Question: You said it went into a water drain? You mean it went into the water system?

Brooks: One of the supervisors took a backhoe and went toward Hunt School and he dug a hole and tried to stop it but he couldn't.
 Normally when we have spills, what the plant manager do #1 [sic]. lock the gates so no reporters can get in. #2 He's gonna take a truck, go to the store somewhere and purchase 400-500 bottles of washing powder. That's why when you pass those ditches, if you ever look in them

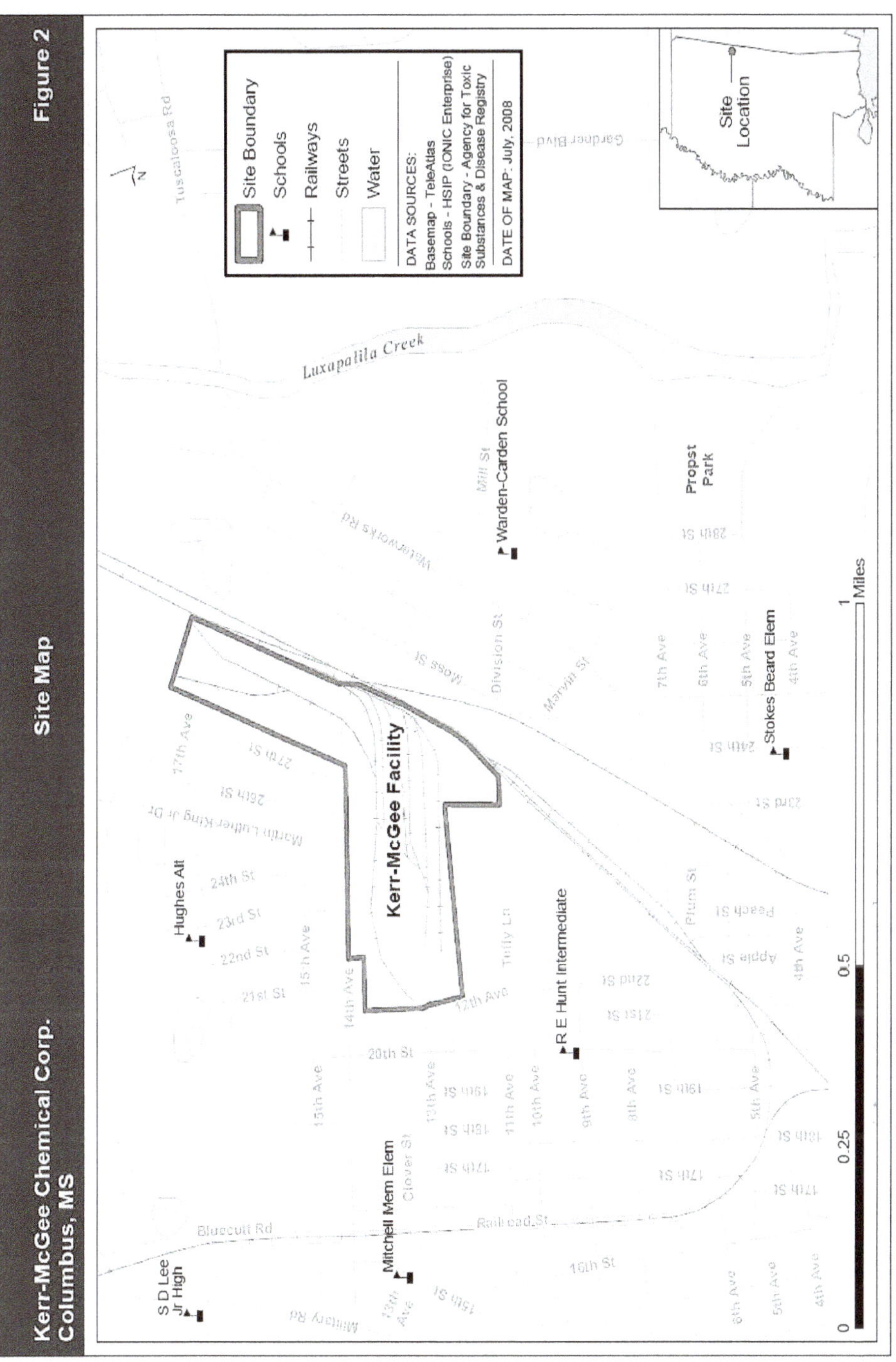

Figure 2. Site Map Showing Site Boundary and Schools Near the Kerr-McGee Facility, U.S. Dept. of Health and Human Services, Public Health Service. 2014. *ATSDR Public Health Assessment for Kerr-McGee Chemical Corporation (a/k/a Tronox, Inc.) Columbus, Lowndes County, Mississippi EPA Facility I.D. MSD990866329 JUNE 12, 2014.* The ATSDR Public Health Assessment, 12. https://www.atsdr.cdc.gov/hac/pha/Kerr-McGeeChemicalCorporation/Kerr-McGee_Tronox,%20Inc_PHA_Final_06-12-2014.pdf

they look white. That's washing powder where they tried to clean it up.

When they pull the crossties out of the cylinders, they supposed to let them crossties sit there on that pad — call them drip pad — that's what it does, catch all the dripping from them crossties. But they say they ain't got time to do that. We lose too much production. So, they'll pull them out the cylinder and take them straight across the road, all the way over on the other side. And that's all you gotta do. All you gotta do is just follow it. Creosote off that drip pad goes all the way across the highway.

Question: You mean across 14 (Avenue)?

Brooks: Across 14, because they don't have time to let it sit there and drip all the dripping off.

Johnny Roberts 5-Year Kerr-McGee Employee

You see the trail, I mean it's like a highway going down, as the water recedes you can just see the black. It's like having water and somebody dripping oil into it. I mean you can definitely see as it recedes, where it is going. And it just pulls, especially freshly treated ties. I mean those (plate) the worst, as they sit there stacked and sitting in the water it's pulled. As it recedes you can see it just goes with the water. With that many ties, you can see through the drainage, that when Kerr-McGee drains it goes into the ditch. You see over the tracks, it be [sic] tubes underneath the tracks. From the main yard goes under the tracks, then goes to the ditches. Everything leads to the ditches at Kerr-McGee. The wood sits on there. Your drainage going to the ditches. That's how it's all designed. It sits on a cup, a high point of the property. Everything is designed to flow off.

Yes, (clears his throat) when they transport the wood tram-locomotive pushes it by trams, transports it by track. There's a ditch on either side of the track as it goes to across the street. It would actually ... the tram would kick off because of rocks or debris or wheels break or mishap. Actually, the tram and all the wood it holds — up to 60 pieces, would go right into the ditch, fall sideways or the empty tram would come back off the tracks, hit and fall, spill whatever is in the tram down into the ditch, on both sides of the street.

Jewelean Lowery 16-Year Kerr-McGee Employee

Had 'em running hot wood straight out the cylinder and it's supposed
to set on the tracks for 48 hours. But they say they needed the order out
real bad, so we had to run the wood.

Chris Pritchard 5-Year Kerr-McGee Employee

You got a mess. That's all you can say. You figure you pushing 200
pounds per square inch on a cylinder that's 8 feet in diameter, 100 feet
long. You do the math on how much pressure is on that bad boy. You
got some kind of polymer rubber type gasket that they put in — that was
probably … one of 'em was probably like three quarter of an inch wide
and probably an inch thick. Push the doors, it's got a locking ring on it.
And on the locking ring it's got wedges so as it goes this way (illustrating
with his hands) the wedge gets tighter and tighter to press the door. But
you had to pay attention because sometimes you can catch it. You can see
when one of the gaskets was getting a bad spot on it before it blowed.

But I have seen times that I'd go out and look at my doors, everything's fine, be walking back — to go walk out the back of the plant
— and all of a sudden, the radio humming, "'Hey, y'all need to cut it off,
you got a gasket blow." Go back and its blown creosote … I mean it's just
bloated. I've seen it blow through the air and travel up to our cars, which
was in the parking lot above it. I've seen it just coat the ground which
was gray rock — all beside it — it's coated the pad out front. It's flowed
against the fuel tanks before. I've seen it sprinkle the framing mill which
was the next building over.

It's just according to what direction the wind is blowing, how long
and how bad it blows. You know if it's got a small crack in it, it don't
blow as bad, if it blows the whole seal in half and then you got it bad
(clears his throat). It's a mess no matter what you do, 'cause then you got
200 degree creosote flying through the air like a mist.

Ben Lowery 18-Year Kerr-McGee Employee

On many occasions that I know it's number 1 cylinder. They had brought
some man from Oklahoma City, somewhere ever he come from, called
himself try to fix the door. Because they put, see the gasket. The door,
the door rim got a gasket in it. Every one to two days the gasket would

blow. If anybody walk across the path, right across the front of the doors, where the gasket blow, creosote gonna burn them. See what I'm saying? Creosote gonna burn them. You know it's gonna get on you anywhere,. Wherever it get on you at, it's gonna burn. It still ... it still whutin right, you know what I'm saying?

Question: So how long did this go on, that the door, the gasket on the door kept blowing and the creosote was coming out into the atmosphere?

Lowery: I know it had been going on about a year.

Question: So you mean for a year at the Kerr-McGee facility, you had creosote gaskets, creosote escaping from cylinder when it was being treated?

Lowery: Yeah and then another thing is that it had got so bad they had to put a light. They had put three lights up there upon the side of the wall on the outside, letting people know, letting employees know that, what cylinder was under pressure and all this. See what I'm saying? They did that because they were afraid the doors were gonna blow, then the creosote was gonna get on some people. You know what I'm saying? Some employees. But that still didn't help though.

Weaseling Out[21]

Having spent more than $1 billion in environmental cleanups in just a few years, Kerr-McGee sought to stem the bleeding by figuring out how to weasel out of its environmental pollution and legacy liabilities. By the end of 2005, Kerr-McGee had settled more than 15,000 lawsuits at a cost of $72 million; all of them involved harmful exposure to creosote contamination. But there were more lawsuits waiting to be settled. There were nearly 9,500 additional lawsuits with $26 million in fees having already been paid.

Five years earlier in 2000, Kerr-McGee had hired Lehman Brothers to develop a plan to help the industrial behemoth avoid paying for permanently polluting America's water supply and possibly exposing hundreds of thousands of people to toxic products that caused cancer and other

---

21   In re *Tronox Incorporated*, No. 09-10156-ALG, at 4-26. (Bankr SDNY, Dec. 12, 2013) http://www.nysb.uscourts.gov/sites/default/files/opinions/180333_622_opinion.pdf.

illnesses. In February 2005, Kerr-McGee hired lawyers at Covington & Burlington — environmental and litigation lawyers — to research fraudulent conveyance litigation in other failed spinoffs. The research lasted for more than three months, but it relieved the worries of Kerr-McGee management to go ahead with the spin-off of the company.

The company formed a new holding company and named it Kerr-McGee Worldwide Corporation, in which it proceeded to put all ownership interest that was currently in the exploration and production branches inside of it. It also simultaneously formed a new subsidiary called Kerr-McGee Chemical Worldwide LLC where Tronox Worldwide LLC would later originate from. The scheme was to dump all the legacy liabilities from Kerr-McGee's original company, including any and all lawsuits for harmful exposure from a chemical, or for chronic disease, cancer, etc. into Tronox and then ensure that Tronox became bankrupt in order to wipe out the liabilities and thus, wash their hands clean. Kerr-McGee did everything in its power to ensure Tronox's bankruptcy by burdening it with heavy monetary obligations and providing it with an inadequate amount of startup money to successfully operate long term. Kerr-McGee celebrated a successful spin-off once Tronox became an independent company.

Once the crippling burdens from its chemical arm were shed, Kerr-McGee was now considered an attractive "Pure Play" company. Less than three months after the spin-off Anadarko Petroleum purchased Kerr-McGee for $16.5 billion cash plus $2.6 billion in debt. It was the deal of the century for Anadarko, scooping up nearly a billion barrels of oil at a fire sale price of approximately $12 a barrel.

Meanwhile, the financial struggle for Tronox was immediate. Due to its heavy financial obligations, the company easily ate through its meager cash pile in the two years after it became an independent company. It filed for Chapter 11 bankruptcy in January of 2009. For a moment it looked like things were going as planned for Kerr-McGee. That is, until the U. S. Federal Government got involved.

Shortly after Tronox filed for Chapter 11 bankruptcy, the federal government intervened against Kerr-McGee under the Federal Debt Collection Practices Act. The United States case was about Fraudulent Conveyance made with the intent to hinder and defraud creditors with 85 years of legacy liabilities when Kerry-McGee dumped all its legacy liabilities into the insolvent Tronox.

Eventually, Tronox was made to take responsibility and settled with the EPA and other federal, state and local agencies and the Navajo Nation. Tronox settled with the federal government for $270 million and 88 percent of Tronox's interest would go toward bankruptcy-created trusts and funds aimed at cleaning up the contaminated sites Kerr-McGee had left across the country. "Because the Tronox locations were so secret, an unknown number of people who may be suffering today would have no way of tracing their ailments to Kerr-McGee." (John Hueston oversaw the legal strategy for the lawsuit and was a federal prosecutor in the trial of Enron Corporation executives Ken Lay and Jeffery Skilling.) Also, "Kerr-McGee took steps to ensure that both the EPA and other potential claimants would not know or discover polluted sites in a timely fashion."[22]

Kerr-McGee's parent company Anadarko Petroleum also settled with the United States Government for $5.15 billion on November 10, 2014 in the U.S. District Court for the Southern District of New York. The historic settlement agreement announced by the EPA and the Department of Justice on April 3, 2014, resolved fraudulent conveyance claims against Kerr-McGee Corporation and related subsidiaries of Anadarko Petroleum Corporation. This settlement was paid with interest to the litigation trust on January 23, 2015.

I want to mention that the judge in this case ruled that the settlement amount should be between $5 billion and $14 billion. The federal government settled this matter for $5.15 billion. I don't know how or why they arrived at that number, but in my opinion it's not nearly enough. With a growing number of future tort claims and new chronic disease manifestations, I fear the money to pay claims will not last long enough to satisfy everyone's settlement. To my knowledge a trust has not been set up to compensate tort claims 10 to 20 years from now. Since we know that disease manifestations are often delayed, how will people pay for their medical treatments in the future?

---

22   "Anadarko Fights Ailing Preacher in $25 Billion EPA Toxic Law Suit", *Newsmax*, May 1, 2012, https://www.newsmax.com/Finance/Markets/Anadarko-Preacher-Toxic-Lawsuit/2012/05/01/id/437649/

Chapter Ten

The Lawsuit

In April 2004 I was already feeling sick. I was vomiting frequently and
I had lost my appetite. I was still running my business, supplying and
installing aluminum entrances and store fronts as well as windows and
skylights around town and on the outer Hawaiian Islands. One morning
I had a meeting with Anna Oshiro, my attorney, about a business-related
matter. We started chatting as we normally did.

"How're you doing, Antonio?"
"I'm feeling sick. Throwing up a lot. I recently found out that I have high
blood pressure."
"That doesn't sound like a normal symptom of high blood pressure. High
blood pressure is usually taken care of with medications," she said while
looking at me with concern. "Do you have a doctor taking care of the
issue for you?"
"Yeah, I'm seeing an internal medicine doctor who takes my blood pressure and a urine sample every time I see him. He has a lab in his office."

Having a lab in a doctor's office was a big deal at the time. I had no idea
that each one of those lab tests showed that the levels of my urine protein along with the levels of my creatinine and levels of microscopic
blood in my urine were gradually increasing. I now know that these are
all markers of kidney disease and they were shouting louder and louder
as I got sicker and sicker.

Shortly after that meeting I started on dialysis. I called Anna, who I had
seen just a few weeks earlier.
"Hi Anna."
"Hi Antonio. How are you doing?"
"I'm not well. I'm on dialysis three times a week. I have end stage renal
failure."
"Antonio, how could you have gone from having high blood pressure to
kidney failure so quickly?" she asked in disbelief. "It sounds like the doctor who is treating you for high blood pressure has been missing something much worse!"
"Well, I don't want to do anything to hurt him. We are both coin collectors
and he often talks to me about the highly valued coins in his collection. I

have a lot of respect for him. Often, when I'm pouring over coins I can't afford at the coin shop, the store owner will ask me to leave because it's close to the doctor's appointment. He told me that whenever the doctor comes in he closes his store just to accommodate him."
"Hey, it's your decision but keep in mind that you're a young man and due to your condition, you may never work again. You'll be on dialysis, very sick and you may never again be able to earn a living or be able to support yourself."

I continued to work for a while with the catheter in my neck. When my foreman first saw it he thought I'd gotten beat up in a fight and that the catheter was a temporary band aid. To him, it was very sudden and appeared overnight. Everyone was shocked to find out that I was on dialysis, including me. I was actually in denial for most of my first year on the machine. My denial was so strong that I actually told my kidney doctor that eventually they will realize what a big mistake they've made and all will have to apologize to me. I was wrong. Many people think that the dialysis process can actually replace a functioning set of kidneys. It can't. The catheter in my neck used to help clean my blood and remove excess fluids was constantly subject to infection. Eventually, the reality of my declining health wore me down.

My lawyer, Anna Oshiro, had a partner who worked in the personal injury field. After some discussion we agreed to have him look at my case and tell me whether or not his investigation could determine whether I had a case or not. The following day I delivered some of my medical records to my attorney's office. I signed a contract with my lawyer's firm to represent me in a malpractice suit against my primary care physician (PCP) in the event that I had a case worth pursuing.

Firstly we had to obtain all of my medical records from Dr. Robertson, my PCP. He was unresponsive to the first, second and third requests from my attorneys for the release of all my medical records. Finally, I received a letter from my lawyer informing me that the doctor was not responding to our requests. I called the doctor's office and spoke with the medical assistant in charge. She agreed to have a copy of all my medical records ready for pick up within 24 hours.

The following afternoon I arrived at the doctor's office. The medical assistant I had spoken with asked me to wait in a private room because the doctor wanted to speak to me. I told her that I was very upset that my lawyers had requested these records three times over a two-month period without a response from their office. I told her I wanted my records NOW! She insisted that I wait until the doctor spoke to me. I waited. The doctor arrived with my records in hand. He nervously asked me,

"Why do you need your medical records?"
"I need to do what's best for me."
"I can assure you that I've done nothing wrong."
"Take a good look at me, doc," I said as I pointed to the catheter in my neck. "If you've done me no wrong then you have nothing to worry about."

He shook his head, handed me my records and walked out. I left his office relieved that I'd finally gotten my records and was ever more determined to set things right.

The next day I delivered my medical records to my lawyer's office and they started in earnest to investigate my case. Their investigator researched my condition of membranoproliferative glomerulonephritis type 2 or MPGN II that was diagnosed by a local pathologist at St. Francis Medical. It is difficult to treat MPGN II since since it's nearly non-responsive to treatment. Even if I had been diagnosed earlier, it most likely would have resulted in kidney failure. I received a crushing phone call from my lawyer who informed me that they could not take my case because I had been diagnosed with incurable kidney disease. The law firm contacted me by mail to confirm that based on the diagnosis I did not have a strong enough case to pursue. They told me that while I had been treated horribly and that it was indeed malpractice, they didn't feel they could win because my kidney disease was incurable. I felt like someone had kicked me in the stomach.

I changed PCPs and kind of bounced around for a while from one physician to another until I found someone I was comfortable with. The nephrologist and the PCP worked together by phone along with a new host of specialists. I eventually needed five doctors, including my nephrologist, PCP and now a cardiologist, an infectious disease doctor and an oncologist.

Eventually I closed my offices and worked with a helper out of my house for a short time until I became too sick to work at all. I moved out of my house and into a YMCA, sold and pawned all the coins in my prized coin collection and even sold all my camera and photography equipment. But I did not give up. I started searching around town for a law firm that would take my case; unfortunately I was unable to find one.

I discovered that malpractice cases are incredibly expensive to pursue. You need to hire experts to testify about everything from the breach of the doctor's standard of care to damages to the particulars of your disease and so on. Even though pretty much everyone agreed that my primary care doctor had really screwed up by waiting too long to refer me to a kidney specialist, with my MPGN II diagnosis and my doctor's negligence, no law firm could see how to recoup sufficient damages to warrant the cost of a trial.

At this point Fumi and I had become close friends. She had a couple of presentations scheduled in New Orleans and I wanted to visit my family, so we decided to meet up in New Orleans for the weekend after my family visit. It was during this trip home when Sereta asked me if there was anything she could do for me. I replied, "Yes! Find me a lawyer who's had successful kidney disease verdicts!" She promptly went online and started looking for lawyers from every part of the country. Later that day she shared what she had found on the internet: Kurzban Kurzban Weinger and Tetzeli, a Miami law firm.

Readying for the Legal Fight

I looked them up online to find that they had recently won a large award for a kidney malpractice case. With spirits high, I thanked her and told her that I was thrilled. When I got back to Hawaii I called Anna Oshiro. I gave her the names and all the information I had on the Florida lawyers. She got in touch with the Florida law office and spoke to Jed Kurzban. Jed confirmed that MPGN II can be an incurable kidney disease. However, he also told her that there is another type of MPGN — MPGN I, a treatable disease — which can be confused with MPGN II. He was very interested in my situation and wanted to fly out to Hawaii after the Christmas holidays. He also wanted to see my medical records and run them by some experts. Anna sent him everything and after review and consultation, the Kurzbans agreed to take my case. Anna would serve as local counsel in the Hawaii courts. I was over the moon.

My first meeting with Marvin Kurzban, Jed's partner and father, was at my lawyer's office in January 2005. When I entered the conference room Anna and Marvin Kurzban were both sitting at the end of a very long, rectangular conference table. Anna introduced me to Marvin who told me that he was very sympathetic to my current condition. He went on to say that things will get better. Marvin was a Miami lawyer who spoke with a booming voice and a Brooklyn accent so strong that he passed it on to his son Jed who had never lived in Brooklyn but sounded as though he'd lived there his whole life.

My attorney Anna Oshiro presented the attorney-client agreement to me. The agreement stated that the firm of Kurzban Kurzban Weinger Tetzeli and Pratt would take my case on contingency. Their fee structure was 30 percent when settled out of court, 40 percent for a case that goes to court and 50 percent if the case is appealed. I signed right away since they were exactly what I had been looking for: experienced lawyers — particularly in the area of kidney disease. I was ecstatic that my search for a good lawyer was over!

I was also informed that a meeting with the Medical Claims Concilia-tion Panel (MCCP) needed to be scheduled because anyone filing a claim against a doctor in the state of Hawaii has to undergo an administrative hearing first.

The MCCP's purpose is to help all parties involved evaluate whether or not a case should be pursued further through the judicial system and to help reconcile deserving cases prior to the parties incurring the substan-tial expenses and time of extended litigation. My feeling is that the MCCP is a useless entity because neither of the parties has to honor the panel's decision and the decision is not even usable in a court of law afterward. I believe that only the attorneys are the winners in an MCCP proceeding. Nevertheless, I was told it was very hard to win an MCCP hearing as the panel tends to favor the doctors. This is likely because doctors make up a large portion of the MCCP panel. For this reason, Jed and Marvin kept their presentation short and sweet.

They did, however, detail how many times I had visited my primary care physician who had run my lab tests at his onsite lab and charging for ev-ery time I came in. He had watched my creatinine level creep up and then leap upward to the point of no return. He did absolutely nothing. He did nothing to stop or even try to slow down my obviously declining health as I slid toward complete kidney failure. Even with this limited presentation we were surprised when we won the MCCP hearing. The judges were unanimous in their decision and voted in our favor regarding liability. My attorneys reached out to the opposing side afterward to ask if they wanted to try to resolve the claim out of court. They did not. A couple of weeks later my attorneys filed the malpractice lawsuit that demanded no specific amount of money.

The opposing counsel assigned to our case was a well-established and very successful insurance defense lawyer from Hawaii. He had a noteworthy record of about 40 tried medical malpractice cases without a loss. In almost every way he was the opposite of Marvin and Jed. The Kurzbans both had loud booming voices, were about 5'6" and broadly built. Tom Cook was very tall, slim and wore well-fitted, trim tailored suits. He had a mild, soft, soothing voice with which he made smooth objections and statements. They were a study in contrast, both in appearance and style.

During the investigative period Marvin Kurzban traveled to every hospital and city I had visited — the Mayo clinic in Minnesota and Northwestern Memorial Hospital in Chicago — to depose several of the doctors who'd treated me. He was a seasoned attorney who focused on unraveling the intricacies of my case. I felt blessed to have him fighting for me.

When he returned to Hawaii we went out to a nice steakhouse for dinner. Marvin ordered a large steak and a glass of wine while I couldn't eat much because I was still sick. Marvin was tired from his travels — the flight from Florida to Hawaii is a very long one — but no meal or conversation with Marvin can end without him recovering his energy and zeal for his work.

Over dinner Marvin explained that he was not going to leave any stones unturned. He instructed me to go to the hospital and pick up my kidney biopsy slides and bring them to him. And so I did. He mailed all of them to the University of Florida's medical center.

It was a few weeks later when Marvin was about to depose one of the physicians who was to serve as an expert witness when he received a shocking call from the University of Florida's kidney pathologist. Everyone had been waiting to hear whether I had a treatable or untreatable form of MPGN. Marvin learned from the pathologist that I didn't have MPGN at all. I had something called Light Chain Deposition Disease (LCDD).

Since then I have learned that LCDD is a rare blood cell disease that occurs when complete or partial monoclonal immunoglobulins are deposited in organs, especially the kidneys. These light chains are used to make antibodies to fight infection and are normally cleared by the kidneys but in LCDD there is an overabundance of these light chains and the kidney becomes overwhelmed, leading to kidney failure. According to my research about half the people with LCDD have what's called a plasma cell dyscrasia, a spectrum of diseases that includes multiple myeloma, a disease I was also diagnosed with.

Stunned by this revelation, Marvin sought a second opinion for confirmation so he sent the kidney biopsy slides to a pathologist at the University of California in Los Angeles (UCLA). UCLA confirmed the LCDD diagnosis.

Marvin's discovery of the MPGN II misdiagnosis — not once but twice — first by the St. Francis Medical Center and then by the University of Utah, was phenomenal and marked a profound turning point in the case as well as my medical treatment.

First, it meant that I could now get the proper treatment for what was ailing me. Second, the new diagnosis drastically changed the projection of my case. Having been diagnosed with LCDD — a disease that could have been prevented from causing end stage kidney disease — instead of MPGN II — a disease that usually progresses to end stage no matter what — Marvin had effectively saved both my case and my life. An early diagnosis along with scheduled Velcade chemotherapy would not only have stopped the further degradation of my kidneys, but dialysis would never have been necessary. In other words, my kidneys could have been saved. Still, it was a matter to be proven in court.

At my lawyer's urging, I scheduled an appointment with a local oncologist to get a third diagnosis of the LCDD in case an oncologist was needed. They wanted my own oncologist to diagnosis my condition correctly in case he was needed for trial. One of the reasons why the LCDD didn't show up in the standard laboratory test is because the light chain assay test was not available for doctors to use until 2007. This by no means implies that LCDD was not being diagnosed until 2007. The University of Florida and the UCLA pathologists both diagnosed LCDD from my kidney biopsy slides using electron microscopy images in 2006. The Mayo Clinic pathologist, using the same kidney biopsy slides presented to them, also made the diagnosis of LCDD during my first visit there.

One of the biggest hurdles for the defense would be this new diagnosis. One of our expert witnesses was Dr. John Goldstein, the director of the Yale Clinical Hematology Laboratory. He, along with Dr. Fumi Horita, my former nephrologist, both testified at deposition and at trial that if there had been an earlier referral to a nephrologist, a renal biopsy would have been ordered and the interpreting pathologist would have diagnosed LCDD. This alone proves that the care I received from my former primary care physician was below the normal standard of care.

LCDD had revealed itself on all my kidney biopsy slides. Marvin Kurzban wondered if the pathologist at the University of Utah, who initially photographed the images had used a poor-quality electron microscopic lens — especially since three different hospitals all diagnosed LCDD on different days.

On March 23, 2007, I underwent a very painful bone marrow biopsy to confirm the diagnosis of multiple myeloma. This procedure was done in a small room where the doctor routinely saw patients. After a discussion with the oncologist about how to proceed I decided to go to the Mayo Clinic because they had expertise in the treatment of multiple myeloma. I told my oncologist that I wanted to get a more thorough diagnosis of everything that was going on with me.

I looked forward to my initial visit to the Mayo Clinic and I have to say that it lived up to its reputation. On my first day at the main entrance outside the Mayo Clinic's Gonda Building, I waited alongside roughly 100 other people for the hospital's doors to be unlocked. When I entered I found myself in the largest medical facility I'd ever seen. It was spotless. I had an appointment scheduled that had been mailed to me about a week prior to my visit. Some of my appointments were at other hospitals on their Methodist campus in downtown Rochester. In 2018, U. S. News & World Report ranked the Mayo Clinic in Rochester, Minnesota first among all US hospitals nationwide. People from all over the world come to the Mayo Clinic for diagnosis and treatment of rare diseases. My schedule consisted of three appointments per day with various doctors and clinics scattered throughout their Methodist campus.

One appointment was with Dr. Sheila Johnson, a kidney transplant nephrologist, who wanted me to undergo a kidney transplant. However, she was unable to convince Dr. Jim Richards, my new hematologist, to approve. He had a different plan of care for me. She totally caught me off guard during my initial visit. I thought it would be like any other routine initial doctor's exam — answering questions and such. There was no mention of a prostate exam and suddenly I'm instructed to drop my pants right there in her office within minutes of meeting her! I was so not prepared for that.

At the end of my first visit to the Mayo Clinic my hematologist gave me the following diagnosis: multiple myeloma, light chain deposition disease and end stage renal disease secondary to LCDD. This would be the fourth and final confirmation that the initial diagnosis of MPGN II was wrong.

Dr. Jim Richards recommended Velcade as the primary chemotherapy drug along with dexamethasone — a corticosteroid that helps offset the negative side effects of chemotherapy. Dexamethasone often gave me the hiccups for about an hour or two after it was administered. The combination of the two drugs worked phenomenally well for me. After three months of treatment in Hawaii I returned to the Mayo Clinic for evaluation and learned that I was in remission but not "stringent complete hematologic remission." Stringent complete means that Velcade has likely given me the best results possible and according to my Mayo Clinic hematologist, the only way to get a stringent complete hematologic remission would be to undergo an autologous stem cell transplant. Dr. Richards was head of the clinic's Autologous Stem Cell Transplant (ASCT) program and he strongly believed that it was the best treatment for me. Because of the high-risk nature (with numerous possible side effects) of the transplant, I decided to consider it as a last resort to save my life. These three months that were among the hardest and most turbulent I had thus far experienced in my life. It was one day dialysis, the next day chemotherapy combined with neuropathy pain almost around the clock. Sometimes in the midst of receiving both treatments five days a week for three months, Fumi actually told me I looked 30 years older.

Though I was relieved when the Mayo Clinic informed me that my health insurance had approved my ASCT, I was very cautious and wanted to know as much as I could about the procedure before moving forward. I wanted to know how long I would have to stay in the hospital and how much it would cost. The attorneys wanted to know the cost so they could better project expenses. The doctors couldn't give me a ballpark figure for how much the procedure would cost, but I found out that the hospital stay could last six months. The Mayo Clinic later informed me that my hematologist had ruled out a kidney transplant and that the ASCT would be the only long-term treatment I would be receiving while being monitored for a year or more prior to being considered for a kidney transplant.

Upon hearing this I immediately requested that all my medical records at the Mayo Clinic be forwarded to Northwestern Memorial Hospital in Chicago for evaluation to be included on their kidney transplant list. This was the only hospital I was still registered with at the time. After St. Francis Medical Center dropped the ball by becoming non-responsive, I made sure to get on at least 3 kidney transplant lists that do many transplants each year. The three facilities I initially registered with were Northwestern, University of California San Francisco and St. Francis.

The attorney of my original primary care physician put forth a defense strategy that was built on my MPGN II diagnosis. The fact that MPGN II inevitably causes kidney failure regardless of any treatment received meant that the internal medicine doctor did not breach the standard of care. If that had remained my diagnosis we would not have had a case because there was nothing that could have been done to alter the course of my fate. This defense strategy went out the window when one of Marvin's experts revealed in a deposition that I did not have MPGN II. This single revelation caused an amazing turn of events. Prior to this revelation my entire case and their defense revolved around the diagnosis and treatment of a disease I did not have. If Marvin and Jed Kurzban had not taken my case, my biopsy slides would never have been sent off for a third or fourth opinion and I most likely would not have been correctly diagnosed. Without a proper diagnosis I would not have received the right treatment for my real ailments and that being the case I might not have had the opportunity to be here to write this book.

It was pretty clear that my disease was treatable if caught in time, but the defense still did not want to settle. Instead, they changed their defense and argued that because I had been diagnosed with multiple myeloma, I would die soon. Therefore, I would only suffer from kidney failure for a short time and would not require a large monetary verdict from a jury.

The defense hired a Dr. Rodney Clay who claimed to be an expert specializing in multiple myeloma at the cost of $10,000 per day. I believe he was paid for a total of five days. He flew to Hawaii to testify that patients diagnosed with multiple myeloma only live between 36 to 40 months. During the trial, Jed Kurzban countered in cross examination that by Dr.

Clay's calculations, I was already dead because I had been living with multiple myeloma for 48 months.

Marvin and Jed stayed the path and relayed my case to the jury. In February 2002, I went to see my PCP, Dr. Joseph Robertson, for a complete checkup after applying for life insurance that was ultimately denied due to an abnormal blood reading on the lab report. The life insurance company had included their lab report of my blood work but it was absent any diagnosis. Had I known how to read the report, I would have known that I was already suffering from kidney disease. However, the internist's notes were absent any diagnosis or treatment other than treatment for hypertension, which can cause kidney disease over many years. According to Dr. Fumi Horita, during the two-and-a-half years following that visit in February 2002 my blood pressure was elevated continually, but not high enough nor long enough to cause kidney disease. I was never tested to find the cause of kidney disease or even treated for it though laboratory results showed that I was developing problems of proteinuria (blood in urine), rising creatinine levels and other signs. No mention was made that I needed to see a nephrologist until mid-2004, after my kidneys had already reached end stage and failed. The internist's notes also repeatedly reflected clinical signs consistent with kidney disease such as constant nausea, vomiting, light-headedness and lack of appetite.

The Trial

We went to trial in the fall of 2008. We told my story to the jury: I had joined the U.S. Army and was stationed in Hawaii for seven of my eight years in the service. I opened a glass construction company three years after leaving the service with an honorable discharge. It was 10 years after opening my glass construction company that I started getting sick. We talked about kidney disease and the markers signaling the presence of the disease and how those markers were repeatedly ignored. The opposing side returned with how unfortunate my situation was and that I had been given a life sentence. However, no one was to blame.

I remember going through the trial during October and November of 2008. Even though I was feeling sick and had to leave the courtroom during my scheduled dialysis treatment days, and continued living at the YMCA without a cent to my name, I was full of hope. Maybe it was because it was an election year and we had just elected the first president of African-American descent but I felt like all things were possible and better days lay ahead. I looked forward to being independent again and not having to rely on friends and family for my most basic needs. At the end of Marvin's closing argument, he read a poem written by one of his clients that relayed how they felt about their injury and how it had affected their life. During the reading Marvin, as well as a couple of jurors, teared up. I remember feeling so grateful that they understood what it was like to live with kidney failure.

Then Tom Cook stood up. He unfolded his long legs and arms and gave a long, careful and smooth closing argument. The courtroom was now packed. Many in attendance were from his firm; they'd come to witness one of the senior founding partners in action. After all, he did have streak of 40 plus successfully tried cases to his reputation. Tom expressed his own sympathy for my condition but firmly reminded the jurors that they had a duty to uphold the law and the law limited what could be done here for a reason. He said it was sad, that it was a tragedy to be stricken by a terrible disease like multiple myeloma but it could not give rise to the liability of his client. The jury was silent and thoughtful after his remarks and we were quiet too.

After Tom returned to his seat Marvin leaned over to Jed and said, "Son, do you want to reply?" This was a first. Marvin had always presented the closing arguments in their cases as well as any rebuttal but Jed was learning and growing, and he leaped at the chance to respond. I saw a baton being handed over at that moment and wondered what Jed would say. He walked over to the Elmo projector machine, took a piece of paper out of his exhibit stack and said to the jury, "They want you to deny Antonio relief because he is, they say, going to die. But this is not what his doctors think." He slapped down the paper on a desk and continued, "According to his doctors at the Mayo Clinic, with proper treatment, Antonio's condition will remain in remission for a very long time." He looked at the jury. "We're not giving up on him. Antonio's doctors aren't giving up on him. Don't you give up on him." It was as if a balloon had popped and everyone's ears had cleared.

We waited for the judge to give his instructions and the jury left for deliberation. They took with them a page to fill out that asked four simple questions:

1. DO YOU THINK THE DOCTOR WAS NEGLIGENT IN HIS TREATMENT OF ANTONIO RICHARDSON? If not, that is the only question to be answered. If yes, go to the question below;
2. DO YOU THINK THE DOCTOR'S NEGLIGENCE WAS A LEGAL CAUSE OF ANTONIO RICHARDSON'S INJURY? If not, then stop here. If yes, go to the question below;
3. WHAT DAMAGES SHOULD BE AWARDED FOR LOSSES CAUSED BY THE INJURY?
4. WHAT DAMAGES SHOULD BE AWARDED FOR PAIN AND SUFFERING CAUSED BY THE INJURY?

Marvin, Jed, Anna and I walked back to Anna's office after the trial. Marvin said to me, "Now we wait." He said that the amount of time the jury deliberates is telling. Very short deliberations usually mean a verdict for the defense. If the deliberation lasts for less than three hours, we're probably in trouble. If the deliberation lasts for three to five hours, it's a good sign. If the jury deliberates for more than five hours, it means there are hold outs and they may be trying to influence one or more jurors one way or another which would be a problem. So the optimal time frame for a jury deliberation is between three to five hours. As we sat waiting in the conference room Marvin regaled us with stories from his past cases.

We were informed that a juror had asked a question of us so we sent someone to pick it up. It was signed by the jury foreman. The question: "Can we have the mock-up aid that showed all the dates Mr. Richardson went to see his doctor?" We immediately sent the mock-up aid that the defense wanted to keep out of the court. One of the defense claims was that I had missed many doctor appointments since I was a working contractor and could not always make it to my scheduled appointments. However, I made up each missed appointment shortly thereafter. Jed had created the aid to show the jury that I had visited the doctor more than 60 times during the two-and-a-half year time frame.

The jury foreman was a naturopath who treats people using alternative medical techniques. We saw people going to her for clarity and to socialize throughout the proceeding. It was clear that she was a kind and good listener; someone who would be open to listening carefully to testimony. We recognized her large, open handwriting on the paper and were hopeful that this was a good sign.

At exactly three hours and five minutes from the time we were excused, we were summoned back to court. The jury had reached a verdict. We walked to the courtroom in silence — our hearts pounding. When we sat down at the trial desk, I looked at Marvin, Jed and Anna and we all quietly joined hands underneath the table. Judge Kim took the jury verdict from the bailiff who had retrieved it from the jury forewoman. In silence he read the form. I saw his head travel down the page, reading each question and answer. It occurred to me that if the jury had awarded nothing and found no liability, there would be nothing to read. I thought about the many things Anna had discussed with me should we not win and how much was riding on the next few seconds. Things go through your head so vividly at such defining moments of our lives while the mundane moments can be a blur a week later. It's interesting how years later those seconds are still so fresh in my mind.

The foreman read the jury's findings.

Was the doctor negligent? Yes!
Was the negligence a legal cause of injury? Yes!
How much did Antonio suffer in financial losses? The jury awarded every penny Marvin Kurzban asked for in his closing arguments.

The judge then asked the jurors who had cast a vote in my favor to stand. The 11 out of 12 jurors who voted in my favor stood up. The judge asked next for the jurors who cast a no vote to stand up. One man stood. The judge dismissed the jurors and everyone stood up. The jurors all had to walk past me as they exited the courtroom and as each one of them walked past me, they stopped and shook my hand and smiled. That is, all except for the one juror who didn't vote in my favor.

CHAPTER ELEVEN

Claims Justice

In September 2011, shortly after I returned to Hawaii from a successful kidney transplant, I couldn't keep from wondering why I had chronic kidney disease and multiple myeloma. These conditions didn't run in my family and I was the only one who had either one of these diseases in my extended family. By the time I finally connected my exposure to Kerr-McGee's environmental contamination with my chronic kidney disease, I found out that I was far behind with filing a compensation claim and that it was too late to be added to any of the ongoing class action lawsuits. I called my childhood friend Terrell to see if he knew anything and sure enough Terrell knew a lot about it because he was a member of a class action suit against Kerr-McGee. Terrell told me there were more than 2,000 members in his class and I should call the trustee of the Tronox Incorporated Tort Claims Trust, Garretson Resolution Group (GRG), to see if I could get listed to file a claim.

After I explained my situation to the Garretson representative, he suggested I hire my own attorney to help me join the class action lawsuit. I took his advice and hired a Honolulu attorney to help me to file a claim for my kidney disease and cancer. The attorney first looked up the current financial situation of the GRG and informed me they were currently underfunded. This was prior to the unprecedented $5.15 billion settlement recovered by the federal government from Anadarko Petroleum, the company that had purchased Kerr-McGee. Terrell went on to inform me that the GRG was telling everyone in his class that because of the additional funding from the settlement, they would be receiving increased settlements.

After the additional funding, there was no need to keep my local attorney since he had completed the task of getting me listed. In addition, the trust had opened up to everyone who had lived in the area to file a claim. The trust sent all correspondence through the mail with simple forms to fill out. Since it was now past the deadline to file a claim in U.S. bankruptcy court by the required bar date of August 12, 2009 everyone else had filed by way of the class action lawsuits. My claim was known as a Future Tort Claim (FTC) because I filed after the bar date since I had only found out about the lawsuits two years after that date. I had no idea at the time that there would be many more post bar dated claims just like mine in the following years.

Sometime in 2015, approximately three years after I first contacted Terrell about getting listed for a settlement, word got out that their checks were about to be mailed. He told me this with much excitement and I told him how happy I was for him. However, unknown to him or any of his class members, another group who had also filed claims for the same type of personal injury from exposure to a harmful substance also filed complaints against his entire class and was seeking to have the entire Mississippi group claim thrown out. They were called the "Avoca Claimants" and they were accusing some of the Mississippi class action lawsuit members of fraud and suggested that an investigation was needed prior to releasing settlement checks to any of them. The GRG, did its own investigation and found no evidence of the Avoca Group's claim to support the accusation of fraud. The trustee filed a motion for instructions asking the court if "it (the trustee) had done the right thing" in approving the Mississippi group's settlement checks.

U.S. bankruptcy Judge Michael E. Wiles of the Southern District of New York presided over this case and I have to say, he's quite impressive. Judge Wiles held that the Avoca plaintiffs had no standing to any of the claims filed by the Mississippi group and that their claims were unfounded (1.) Judge Wiles wrote, "The Avoca Group claims were all asbestos claims in category D, Non-Asbestos Toxic Exposure that totaled $966 million or of the 4,400 people who filed claims from that group, the payments on their claims were going to be significantly affected by the allowance of the Mississippi groups claims, which totaled nearly $140 million." (2.) "The Avoca plaintiff's argument against the Mississippi claimants should have never been permitted and that no instructions should have been necessary. They argued that the Mississippi claimants did not file the proper proofs of claim in the bankruptcy case, but instead filed a 'group' claim that should have not been permitted; that only some of the Mississippi claimants had asserted personal injury claims in the 'group' claim that was filed; that the individual Mississippi claimants who held 'nuisance' claims should have been barred from filing trust claims based on illness, disease or other personal injury; and that the claims filed by the Mississippi claimants against the trust are so different in number, nature and dollar value from those described in the bankruptcy proof of claim that a further investigation should be made as to whether fraud was committed."

I'm sure the judge's response was quite a surprise for the GRG because it amounted to a scolding. Judge Wiles also wrote (3.) The court has some skepticism as to whether the motion before this court is an appropriate request for instructions. Ordinarily a trustee seeks instructions when it has not yet taken action and where the trustee is unsure as to what to do and possibly face liability for an incorrect choice. Noting that a 'Request For Instructions' for judicial relief involving a trust can be appropriate in many circumstances, including when the trust agreement is "genuinely ambiguous." He noted that trust instructions proceedings are a well-established procedure by which trustees (and other affected parties) can seek judicial guidance from the court about how best to interpret governing documents. Here the trustee had already taken action. The trustee had allowed the Mississippi claims several years ago, but now had misgivings about the determination it made. In this regard the trustee's motion seems to be mainly a request for "comfort" as to the actions already taken, rather than truly a request for "instructions" as to what the trustee should do going forward in administering the trust. Judge Wiles went on to state that, (4.) "The Avoca plaintiffs have no standing to object to the Mississippi claims and in any event, their objections to the claims are unfounded."[23]

The Avoca plaintiffs later unsuccessfully sued their lawyers, who in my opinion did an excellent job, for more than $600 million — what they claim was the difference lost in their settlement. They managed to recover $330 million for 4,400 members of their group. The group wanted the entire value of the over-inflated schedule of value which amounted to almost a billion dollars — a good deal more than what the entire trust was worth. The Mississippi group was paid $140 million for approximately 2,690 people.

Earlier, Jerry Terrell Petty gave testimony that he and other members of the class had received very little money. Jerry, as well as his fellow class members, are currently being represented by the Tollison Law Firm based in Oxford, Mississippi. He says whenever he calls up the law firm to ask when he will be receiving the remainder of his settlement money, he's told that a conflict has arisen between Tollison and the class's prior lawyer, Howard Gunn. It's likely that the disagreement revolves around the sum of money that's owed to Gunn based on the agreement made when the suit was transferred to Tollison just prior to Gunn's retirement.

---

23   In re *Tronox Incorporated*, No. 09-10156-mew, at 8. (Bankr SDNY, Dec. 14, 2016) http://www.nysb.uscourts.gov/sites/default/files/opinions/175219_3268_opinion.pdf.

The matter has yet to be settled. Jerry Petty also says he and other class members never signed an attorney-client agreement with the Tollison Law firm. Howard Gunn was the lawyer who had signed all the members of the class to the lawsuit and he is the only attorney that Petty and his class members have an agreement with yet the small checks he has received to date were made out by the Tollison Law firm. Perhaps an outside attorney is needed to obtain the funds the federal government meant to go to the people because it's fast approaching three years since the trust first released those funds. The people of Mississippi are tired, sick, frustrated and have been treated very unfairly by their own hired attorneys.

Future Tort Claims

The rational thinking was that if you had a personal injury or medical problem such as cancer, kidney disease or heart failure that was related to or caused by creosote, you were going to get a settlement. Justice or some part of justice is how it *should* be settled though it didn't necessarily mean a settlement would be received. Once a Garretson Resolution Group employee explained this to me, I realized that that wasn't the way things worked.

The trustee, GRG, seemed frustrated with the growing number of future tort claims (FTC). It concocted a devious new plan to limit qualified applicants from filing future tort claims.

It was clearly understood that every claim to be paid for pain, suffering, chronic disease, cancers and a host of other illnesses that had manifested from harmful exposure due to Kerr-McGee's negligence, were to be paid from one of the established categories the Tronox bankruptcy reorganization plan created: Indirect Environmental Claims, Asbestos Claims, Property Damage Claims and Asbestos Toxic Exposure Claims. The new plan changed the name of the four sub-categories to the following: Allowed Indirect Environmental Claims, Allowed Asbestos Claims, Allowed Property Damage Claims and Allowed Asbestos Toxic Exposure Claims. This renaming scheme was just the beginning of a series of attacks against FTC by the trustee Garretson Resolution Group and its attorneys, who sought to limit the inclusion of qualified people who wanted to file valid claims for their injuries. The trust made it clear that only claims that fell into those categories were claims that were the subject of "Proofs of Claims" prior to the August 12, 2009 bar date, or were the subject of proofs of claims that the court had authorized to be filed late through a final order.[24]

The trust was now creating its own defense to hold on to as much of the funding as possible. One has to keep in mind that the residents of Columbus, Mississippi and everywhere else had long been waiting to get some type of justice from Kerr-McGee's contamination of their neighborhoods. Even though the federal government had funded the purse with nearly $600 million to compensate residents who had suffered injury, the trustee now wanted to deny them any type of justice; even if it meant committing fraud to do so. I can't help but wonder where the Garretson Resolution Group attorneys were when they changed the subcategory names simply to prevent qualified future tort claims from being filed and processed.

The trust had not yet finished building its arsenal of weapons to disqualify future tort claims (FTC). I suspect that the following scenario possibly reveals where the trust's attorneys became involved.

In its second and final attempt to rid itself of future tort claims, the Tronox bankruptcy trustee, Garretson Resolution Group, filed a motion in U.S. Bankruptcy Court Southern District of New York. The motion asked the court for instructions regarding the definition of "future tort claims," while giving the court its own definition. This meant excluding everyone who failed to file a proof of claim by the August 12, 2009 bar date. I was in total disbelief when I received the motion. In fact, I was angry and fired up. I was certain that the trustee wanted to keep the remainder of the funding the federal government had supplied to compensate the injured parties. Clearly Garretson Resolution Group sought to keep the money for some use other than compensating people filing future tort claims.

I remembered the name of an EPA attorney and advisor, Melissa Gibbons, at the end of the Tronox bankruptcy summary I had read. I emailed a letter to her explaining the new motion the GRG and its lawyers had submitted to the court. I also explained to her that if this motion were approved, the residents of Morningside Apartments should be exempt since the apartments were built on federal land that was contaminated at the time of occupancy. She gave me an indirect response about a week later.

---

24   The final deadline for a Proof of Claim for debts owed could be filed in court for this bankruptcy.

I received a letter from the trustee's attorneys Keating Muething & Klekamp PLL. They wanted me to write a letter to explain why I believed that their motion should not be approved. I was also told to send one letter to them and a second letter to the bankruptcy court. This really excited me because I had a story to tell.

Here's my letter:

United States Bankruptcy Court, Southern District Of New York
One Bowling Green, New York, NY 10004-1408

Re: Tronox Incorporated, Reorganize Debtors Chapter 11 case No. 09-10156

Opposition to Motion of Tort Claims Trustee, Garretson Resolution Group, Incorporated For Instructions Regarding Future Tort Claims.

To whom it may concern,

I am opposing this motion due to the fact that it violates the Civil Rights Act of 1964 Title VI. 42 U.S.C. that was enacted as a part of the landmark Civil Rights Act of 1964. It prohibits discrimination on the basis of race, color and national origin in programs and activities receiving federal financial assistance.

President Kennedy said in 1963 that simple justice requires that public funds, to which all taxpayers of all races (colors, and national origins) contribute, not be spent in any fashion which encourages, entrenches, subsidizes or results in racial (color or national origin) discrimination.

All the past residents of Morningside Apartments fall under the 1964 Civil Rights Act Title VI in that environmental discrimination was the reason for knowingly building Morningside Apartments on contaminated soil. The apartment complex was one of the original government-supplement programs rolled out by HUD, as part of the Civil Rights Act of 1968. The private owner of Morningside Apartments knowingly and willfully built the apartments on land already contaminated with creosote. The water was also contaminated at the time of occupancy. Additionally Morningside Apartments was financed and insured by the FHA.

Should this motion be approved, and the people pray that it won't, it would kill an opportunity for the federal government to make good on a situation they likely wish they would have treated differently.

Morningside Apartments was a 12-building, two-story complex located on the north side of Columbus, Mississippi, sitting a few blocks from the now closed Kerr-McGee chemical plant. Three smaller single-story buildings were used for office space. The 120 apartment complex consisted of 8-one bedroom, 60-two bedrooms, 48- three bedrooms, and 4- four bedroom apartment units. They were built to house poor black families who had no idea whatsoever that this despicable horror was festering underneath them. The developers in Columbus, Mississippi didn't stop there. They continued to build an entire subdivision on contaminated land on the north side neighborhoods surround Morningside Apartments.

Our family moved to Morningside Apartments in the summer of 1970 when it opened. We moved away sometime in 1973 or 1974. The water that flowed from the faucets inside the units was always a light brown color, so we had to let it run for a few seconds until it was clear. A few times a month the air was strong with a tar smell for most of the day. I lived there while I was in elementary school for the second, third and fourth grades. Additionally, Kerr-McGee stored baked creosote inventory just beyond the Morningside Apartments playgrounds. We, as kids, would play on the stuff and get creosote all over us.

According to documents I've obtained by way of the Freedom of Information Act, Morningside Apartments lost its FHA insurance in 1990 and was foreclosed in 1997. Residents were relocated prior to closing the 12-building complex and eventually all 12 buildings were demolished. The federal government sold the land back to the city of Columbus, Mississippi for $1. Residents were told that all the existing homes surrounding the site where Morningside Apartments existed were to be bought for demolition.

This motion is unconscionable, demeaning and shows no compassion for people who are sick and whose lifespan has been shortened by incurable diseases. Shame on everyone who supports this motion. Is this really how you want to be remembered?

I've lived in Hawaii since joining the U.S. Army in 1981. I started dialysis in 2004. I received a kidney transplant in 2011. In 2006 I was diagnosed with Multiple Myeloma. Sometimes I would be on dialysis one day and chemotherapy the next day for a couple of months. I was diagnosed with osteoporosis in 2013. I was told this was quite common in kidney disease patients. I never knew anything about the name Tronox or its bankruptcy until 2011. I was here in Hawaii fighting for my life.

Sincerely,
Antonio Richardson

The Hearing Regarding Future Tort Claims (October 25, 2016)[25]

Natalie Ramsey of Montgomery McCracken Walker & Rhodes was the first to testify. She was negotiating and drafting the provisions of the bankruptcy reorganization plan and all matters concerning the tort claims. She wanted to make sure that all tort claims were sent through the trust so that a reorganized Tronox would be free of legacy liability. She also testified that the reason the definitions were changed was because a disease would often not appear or manifest until long after exposure. The court questioned Ms. Ramsay about the category of "Future Tort Claims." Ms. Ramsey described it like this:

- *Claims by people who were first exposed to a harmful product after the effective date of the Plan (Transcript, October 25, 2016, at 10:20-11:3.) However, Ms. Ramsey was unable to explain how such a claim would have "arisen" prior to the effective date (which appears to be a requirement of the modified definition), and suggested that in this respect the parties may have been inexact in the words they chose.* Id. *at 11:4-11:22.*

- *Claims by people who were exposed to substances prior to the effective date but whose disease or injuries did not manifest themselves until after the Bar Date.* Id. *at 11:23-12:14.*

- *Claims by people whose symptoms had manifested themselves prior to the Bar Date, but who contend they were not aware of the Bar Date or of the bankruptcy cases to the extent such claimants were successful in arguing that they did not receive sufficient notice as a matter of due process.* Id. *at 12:15-13:15*

---

25   In re *Tronox Incorporated*, No. 09-10156-mew at 1-3. (Bankr SDNY Jan. 19, 2017). http://www.tronoxtorttrust.com/Portals/17/Tronox%20FTC%20Court%20Order.pdf.

> · *Claims by people whose symptoms had manifested themselves prior to the Bar Date and who seek, after the Effective Date, to file late claims on the grounds of "excusable neglect" under Rule 9006 of the Federal Rules of Bankruptcy Procedure.* Id. *at 13:16-14:6.*

See also id. *at 15.7-15:17. Ms. Ramsey also testified, however, that at the time the Plan and related documents were drafted the parties believed that all tort claims would likely have already manifested themselves, and did not expect that there would be a substantial number of future claimants.* Id. *at 15:23-16:8.*

I take issue with Ms. Ramsey's last comment. Kerr-McGee had reigned for over 70 years and had a documented history of failing to clean up its massive environmental contamination across the nation. Why on earth would an attorney, of all people, who has been selected to create the trust documents that govern claims, conclude that all tort claims would have already manifested and would not expect such a large turnout of future tort claims? Shouldn't she have known or at least budgeted for a small percentage of tort claims? It's shameful for Ms. Ramsey to testify that at the time she and her team created the bankruptcy reorganization plan they believed all tort claims would have likely manifested. How in the world can anyone ever predict how many new diseases would be diagnosed during that time frame? But to assume that none would manifest, then overshoot the numbers on the schedule of values and give away the lion's share of the funding provided by the federal government to just a few thousand people, based solely on this wrong assumption is neglectful and highly irresponsible.

Nicole Greenblatt of Kirkland & Ellis LLP testified next. Ms. Greenblatt confirmed one of Ms. Ramsey's testimonies about the various types of claims that should comprise Future Tort Claims. She did so only under questioning from the court. She also testified that "the parties" never thought exposure to the harmful substances would be possible following bankruptcy proceedings because contamination occured years earlier and remediation programs had been planned out. Ms. Greenblatt agreed the claims were and should be considered Future Tort Claims. This is another attorney testifying to Ms. Ramsey's incorrect assumptions when creating the bankruptcy reorganization plan.

Joseph Bruemmer from the Garretson Resolution Group was the third and final person to testify. He gave testimony about how many Future

Tort Claims they had received and said that 2,800 of those claims were diseases that had only manifested after the Bar Date. That is, 2,800 new injuries or diseases had been diagnosed since this hearing took place, from the bar date of August 12, 2009 through December 2016. You have to wonder how many additional injuries/diseases have been diagnosed to date and how many additional injuries/diseases will be diagnosed in the coming years with little or no funding available to settle those claims.

Judge Michael Wiles responded to the Garretson Resolution Group's request for instructions regarding "Future Tort Claims". Judge Wiles wrote, *"A claim qualifies as a future tort claim if it does not fall into the other categories of tort claims and if one or more of the following conditions are met;*

1. The claim is based on an alleged exposure to a harmful substance that occurred on or after August 12, 2009;

2. The claim is based on an exposure that occurred before August 12, 2009, but as to which no injury or disease was manifested until on or after August 12, 2009; or

3. The exposure, as well as the manifestation of an injury or disease, predated August 12, 2009, but the claimant is able to establish (a) that the claimant's failure to file a timely proof of claim should be excused on grounds of excusable neglect,[26] (b) that the purported discharge of the claimant's claim was a violation of due process and therefore ineffective.

Determinations as to claims that fall into categories (1) and (2), above, will be made by the Trustee pursuant to the TDPs and subject to the dispute resolution procedures that are set forth in the TDPs. Claimants in category (3) who wish to obtain relief will be required to file motions seeking such relief from this Court.

Judge Wiles moved to further tear down the trustee's defenses and other issues that were of utmost importance. He started with refusing to limit a tort claim based on the trustee's assertion that a future tort claim was to be based on exposures that occurred only prior to the effective date of Tronox's bankruptcy plan. Next, the judge addressed the trustee's desire to notify the injured whose disease had manifested prior to the bar date

---

26   Excusable neglect basically means the claimant was unaware of the class-action suit until after the bar date had passed.

that their claims were discharged, or not valid. The judge's concern was that by using this approach, it would suggest to the injured people that the court had already made a decision and no due process was available. The truth, in fact, was that the court would be accepting arguments made based on excusable neglect even if the trustee had already denied their claim. Finally, Judge Wiles addressed the trustee's suggestion of imposing a filing fee for appeals. The trustee wanted to charge a $250 filing fee in order to ward off what it called frivolous appeals and litigation that would be refunded upon a successful appeal by any claimant. The trustee had originally proposed to inform people — whose claims were based on exposures that predated the bar date — that their claims had been thrown out. The proposed appeal fee was intended for claimants who wished to contest such discharge, knowing full well that there would be no way the claimants could win. Judge Wiles denied this fee request. These were all a part of the trustee's arsenal of defenses against people who were stricken with chronic disease, cancer and a long host of other illnesses through Kerr-McGee's negligence.

It is likely that many claims were rejected based on the fact that they were filed after the bar date. In fact, in many instances the trustee was outright denying many qualified claimants from even filing by simply denying their requests to file by mail as it happened to a good number of people I know, including my family members.

Judge Wiles then directed the trustee to submit revised forms that reflect these rulings. Firstly, the form of notice to anyone wanting to file a claim should include a proposed description of the categories of claims that may constitute "Future Tort Claims". Secondly, the forms should include a brief explanation of the claimants rights to (A) argue that their failure to file a timely proof of claim should be excused on grounds of excusable neglect, or (B) that the purported discharge of the claimants claim was a violation of due process and therefore ineffective. Those descriptions should include brief statements as to the showings that claimants must make in order to obtain relief from the bar date and/or the discharge order.

Now that everything had been exposed and was out in the open, it was evident that the attorneys who created the trust documents that mainly governed the claims payout process, grossly erred by not accounting for: first and most importantly, new disease manifestation; second, zero future tort claims beyond the August 12, 2009 bar date. Also with the new information explained to the court, there were 19,000 new Future Tort Claims and 2,800 new disease manifestations. Judge Wiles' 2016 ruling on the hearing opened up the claims process to more people who deserve settlements.

In that light, I find it unthinkable for the trustee to NOT properly adjust what seems like a well over-inflated schedule of values prior to sending out the first group of claims checks. What were they thinking? What we do know is this hearing took place on or about October 25, 2016. The two class action lawsuits whose claims were paid first, because of their timely proofs of claim submitted. They received approximately $470 million of the $600 million purse the federal government funded to the trust. This sum went to only 6,690 claimants with the Mississippi group receiving approximately $140 million and the Avoca group receiving approximately $330 million.

Today, the trust has no clearly defined number of how many people will be seeking claims. The Avoca group alone has more than 50,000 future tort claims. It is believed that the FTC value stands somewhere in the hundreds of thousands as the number of claimants steadily continues to grow. The checks started going out in 2016 and stopped mid-2018 and have yet to start up again.

When you call and ask the Garretson Resolution Group when the settlement checks might start up again, they will likely tell you as they told me, "Once everyone is accounted for the settlement checks will start up again. How will they determine when everyone has been accounted for? This is a work in progress that just keeps growing and growing so it could take a decade or more before the remainder of the settlement checks are mailed. You may wonder why they are doing this? I fear there's not enough money left in the purse and this may be the reason why the settlement checks have been put on hold.

It's important to note that in 2015 "The trustee hired NERA Economic Consulting [in 2015] to estimate the number and value of expected new claims, and it projected the trust would receive another 3,385 new claims from 2015 to 2050."[27] With this projection — though grossly underestimated in hindsight — the trust still moved forward without setting aside

---

27   Jennifer Learn-Andes, "Health claims piling up against Kerr-McGee, owner of former Avoca plant", *The Dallas Post, Feb. 1, 2018* https://www.mydallaspost.com/news/local/31655/claims-pile-up-for-people-alleging-health-problems-from-kerr-mcgee-wood-processing-site-in-avoca-and-elsewhere

any funds for new disease manifestation or FTC.

While the door is still open to file a future tort claim, I'm afraid that door may soon close. Yes, it's unfair, especially considering how disease manifestation from harmful chemical exposure can take decades. According to the information GRG is giving by phone, if you turned down the $5,000 offer from them, which I did, then your claim rests in the court's hands. It would seem they are struggling with the increasing number of people filing claims vs. how much money is available for pay out. We all hope for additional funding from the federal government. One thing I am sure of is that we can all expect much smaller payouts than the first two groups who have already received settlements.

As of February 2018 there was $25 million left in the trust but GRG has since paid itself $9 million out of that balance.[28] It appears the GRG made no attempt to adjust the schedule of values to accommodate the tens of thousands of new claimants.

---

28   Ibid

EPILOGUE

Morningside Apartments in Columbus, Mississippi was closed in 1997 once the federal government discovered the grounds were contaminated with creosote. People were relocated or given payouts to move. Once the projects were emptied they were demolished. Later the federal government sold the land back to the city of Columbus for $1.00.

Today, that parcel is still contaminated. A chain link fence encloses the site. A fire department sits on a slab where the laundromat used to be next to the apartments. Although cleanup is ongoing within Columbus, Mississippi. There is a direct focus on cleaning up the many ditches scattered about Columbus. Cleanup is estimated to still take a good number of years before completion.

It has been nearly a year since the GRG trust has stopped awarding additional monies and no one knows when they will restart. Occasionally I call the Garretson Resolution Group for an update on the situation. They ask for identifying information and once I've disclosed this information and I'm confirmed as a claim holder, the operator always responds: "That you're waiting for a letter of execution from the court that will have your settlement amount on it."

In the meantime, if you have a creosote- or Tronox-related injury, contact:
The Garretson Resolution Group
6281 Tri- Ridge Boulevard, Suite 300
Cincinnati, Ohio 45140.

Or call 1-800-753-2480 to file a Future Tort Claim.

The address for the bankruptcy court is:
United States Bankruptcy Court
Southern District of New York
One Bowling Green
New York, NY 10004-1408

Contact Judge Michael E. Wiles.

Just prior to publishing, in August of 2019, Anadarko Petroleum was acquired by Occidental Petroleum for $38 billion.

Epilogue

I recommend that people call and write to their Senator and Representative about the urgent need to set up a 70-year trust to be funded annually by the federal government to pay for future tort claims. This is so very important since we have learned that disease from harmful exposure can, and in many instances, will be delayed and will manifest itself sometime later in life. That is why it's so important that the federal government, having recovered more than $5 billion from Anadarko, continue to fund the trust for decades.